YORK NOTES

General Editors: Professor A.N. Jeffares (*University of Stirling*) & Professor Suheil Bushrui (*American University of Beirut*)

William Wordsworth

SELECTED POEMS

Notes by P.H. Parry

BA (BRISTOL) MA (BIRMINGHAM) PH D (ST ANDREWS)
Lecturer in English, University of St Andrews

LONGMAN
YORK PRESS

YORK PRESS
Immeuble Esseily, Place Riad Solh, Beirut

LONGMAN GROUP UK LIMITED
Longman House, Burnt Mill, Harlow,
Essex CM20 2JE, England
Associated companies, branches and representatives
throughout the world

First published 1982
Seventh impression 1992

ISBN 0-582-03369-1

Printed in Hong Kong
WC/05

Contents

Part 1

Introduction

The life of William Wordsworth

William Wordsworth was born, the second in a family of five, in 1770 in Cockermouth, an ancient and small market-town set in comparatively flat countryside to the north-west of that 'district of the Lakes in the North of England' with which his reputation is now most closely associated. His mother, Ann, was the daughter of a Penrith tradesman; his father, John, was law-agent to Sir James Lowther (later Earl of Lonsdale), a political magnate of immense wealth but an eccentric and unreliable employer. It was Sir James who provided the extremely fine house in which all five of the Wordsworth children were born: Richard in 1768, Dorothy in 1771, John in 1772, and Christopher in 1774.

Wordsworth received his earliest formal education in a small school in Penrith (where he studied alongside Mary Hutchinson, whom he was eventually to marry) and in the grammar school in Cockermouth. In 1778, while the children were staying with her at her father's house in Penrith, Ann Wordsworth, who was only thirty-one years old, died. Rather than have his children return to him, John Wordsworth agreed that they should stay with their grandfather. Dorothy, however, was soon separated from her brothers and sent to live with cousins in Halifax. At Whitsuntide 1779 Richard and William were entered at Hawkshead Grammar School which, though small, especially by modern standards, was well known and provided a good education. They lodged, first in Hawkshead itself, later in the neighbouring hamlet of Colthouse, with Hugh and Anne Tyson, of whom William became very fond. In 1782, John, and in 1785, Christopher also entered the school and lodged with the Tysons. In 1783 the elder John Wordsworth, whom his children cannot have known intimately, died.

The early loss of his parents and the enforced absence of his sister, which both he and Dorothy greatly resented, help to explain the strong emphasis upon family relationships that is a characteristic feature of Wordsworth's verse. He soon had other reasons for thinking about families and family responsibilities.

In 1787 Wordsworth left Hawkshead and proceeded to St John's College, Cambridge. His university career was undistinguished, but, though he seems not to have been industrious in pursuing formal studies, he read English poetry widely, wrote a little, and began to learn Italian. The Long Vacation of 1789 he spent at Penrith with his sister and Mary Hutchinson; that of 1790 he gave over to continental travel, and in the company of a fellow student, Robert Jones, crossed the Alps—an event which affected him deeply and which he records in Book VI of *The Prelude*. After graduation, early in 1791, Jones and he toured North Wales which was then, like the Lake District and the Wye Valley, a favourite haunt for travellers in search of picturesque landscape.

In November 1791 Wordsworth returned to France, a country already disturbed by revolutionary change and soon to be disturbed even more thoroughly. Though his sympathies were at this time republican, in Orleans, where he went in order to learn French, he met and fell in love with Annette Vallon, a young woman four years older than he, and of a royalist family. She bore him a daughter, Caroline, in 1792.

It had been decided that Wordsworth should enter the ministry of the Church of England, which was considered to be perfectly normal employment for a young graduate who had no other prospects. With this idea in mind he returned to England late in 1792, but, in the light of the French scandal, which Wordsworth did not seek to conceal, an uncle who had offered to help to further his ordination plans withdrew his offer, with the result that his nephew put aside for ever thoughts of becoming a clergyman.

Though his domestic life was unsettled, Wordsworth was beginning to make his mark as an author: in 1793 both *An Evening Walk* and *Descriptive Sketches* 'taken during a pedestrian tour in the . . . Alps' were published. They were read and admired by Samuel Taylor Coleridge (1772–1834), then not known to Wordsworth, but soon to become the most famous of all his acquaintances. The likelihood of Wordsworth's being able to marry Annette was not great, and lessened as relations between England and France grew worse. Eventually he gave up all thoughts of the match, but there was no breach between them, and Wordsworth was able to remain on friendly, or at least composed, terms with both mother and daughter.

His financial situation, which was not good and which was made worse by Lord Lonsdale's withholding payments owed to Wordsworth's father, was eased in 1795 when Raisley Calvert, younger brother of a Hawkshead school-friend, died and left him a legacy of £900. In this same year Wordsworth visited Bristol and there, for the first time, met Coleridge, and also Robert Southey (1774–1843) and Joseph Cottle. The former, a native of the city, was a poet with whom Wordsworth and Coleridge were to be closely associated; the latter was the man who first printed *Lyrical Ballads*. Wordsworth then went to Racedown, in Dorset, where he and Dorothy were, with the help of Calvert's legacy, able to set up house. It was while he was living at

Racedown that *The Borderers*, his only play, was written.

In June 1797 Coleridge visited the Wordsworths, staying with them for a few weeks. This visit was such a success, and impressed the Wordsworths so much, that they decided to move to Alfoxden House, in Somerset, in order to be near Nether Stowey where Coleridge was living with his family. One consequence of this move, and of a short walking holiday that followed it, was the planning of *Lyrical Ballads* by the two poets. In July 1798 Wordsworth and Dorothy visited Tintern Abbey, which Wordsworth had first seen in 1793. The famous 'Lines, Composed a few miles above Tintern Abbey' were written down as soon as Wordsworth returned to Bristol, in time to be included in the first edition of *Lyrical Ballads*, published anonymously in September 1798. Within a few days of its publication Wordsworth, Dorothy and Coleridge set sail for Germany, the Wordsworths staying in Goslar, in Saxony, throughout a bitterly cold winter, and Coleridge in Göttingen.

In the spring of 1799 Wordsworth and Dorothy returned to England and stayed with Mary Hutchinson and her parents in County Durham. In December the Wordsworths moved into the former Dove and Olive Branch Inn at Town End in Grasmere, a cottage which Wordsworth had noticed when on a walking tour with Coleridge in November. This return to his 'dear native regions' was final, for though a considerable traveller, both abroad and in his own country, Wordsworth never again set up house outside the Lake District.

The eight years which Wordsworth spent at Dove Cottage were amongst the happiest of his life, and are vividly depicted in his sister's journals. During these years he completed a thirteen-book version of *The Prelude*, and began *The Excursion*, another very long poem. *Lyrical Ballads*, to which he added a second volume, went through three further editions; and in 1807 he published *Poems in Two Volumes*, which, though not well received at the time, contains some of his best known shorter work. Nor were his achievements exclusively literary: in 1802 he married Mary Hutchinson (1770–1859). While they were living at Dove Cottage three children were born—John in 1803, Dora in 1804, and Thomas in 1806. Only one incident blotted the happiness of these years; in 1805 Captain John Wordsworth, William's favourite brother, was lost at sea.

In 1808, Dove Cottage being too small for the growing family and its frequent visitors, the Wordsworths moved to Allan Bank, a new house and one which they never liked. There, in 1808 and 1810, Catharine and William Wordsworth were born. In 1811 the family moved a short distance to Grasmere's former vicarage, where, in 1812, both Catharine and Thomas died. To escape these bad memories the Wordsworths moved, in 1813, to Rydal Mount, a house midway between Grasmere and Ambleside. Shortly before making the move Wordsworth received from Lord Lonsdale, successor to the man who had withheld payment, the promise of the Distributorship of Stamps for Westmorland. This minor civil service post brought in some much-needed income which was not relinquished until 1842 (when the Distributorship was passed on to the younger William Wordsworth). In 1814 *The Excursion* was published.

From the point of view of the literary historian the last thirty years of Wordsworth's life were uneventful. He continued to write, and revised much of what he had already written, including *The Prelude*, which he altered extensively between 1829 and 1835. His reputation as a poet, once the subject of controversy, was by this time well established, and led to his receiving the conventional rewards of success: honorary degrees (from the Universities of Durham, in 1838, and of Oxford, in 1839) and, on the death of Robert Southey in 1843, the office of Poet Laureate. Inevitably, however, the abiding impression is of a life moving towards its close, its major triumphs in the past. Coleridge, always a difficult friend but a friend nevertheless, died in 1834. In the following year Dorothy, whose relationship with her brother had always been close and intense, suffered a mental decline that left her an invalid for the remaining twenty years of her life. Dora Wordsworth, who had married in 1841, died in 1847.

Wordsworth died in 1850. 'The last poetic voice is dumb' wrote Matthew Arnold. But it was not quite dumb, for after Wordsworth's death his family felt itself able to release *The Prelude*, the poem in which, half a century earlier, he had described the growth of a poet's mind. This poem, which he had never entirely put aside and which illuminates everything else that he wrote, is today the best reason that we have for being interested in the details of Wordsworth's life and of the use which he made of them in his poems.

Literary background

William Wordsworth was born in 1770, when the Romantic movement was in its infancy, and died in 1850, by which time the Victorian age was thirteen years old. Quite apart from the excellence of his verse Wordsworth is worth studying because, alone of all the major English Romantic poets, he spans this transition between the Romantics (of both the first and second generations) and their Victorian successors.

Romanticism is the name given to an extraordinary explosion of interest in all of the arts, and throughout most of Europe, that took place late in the eighteenth century and early in the nineteenth—precise dates are difficult to give and vary from art to art and from country to country. In effect it was another Renaissance (of which there have been several in the history of Western art and thought). Like these previous renaissances Romanticism rejected the artists and thinkers of the recent past for being unduly conventional, or creatively timid, or merely academic; at the same time it reached back further into the past for examples and precedents. Thus in the visual arts (painting, sculpture, architecture and interior decoration) the Romantic movement witnessed a revival of interest in the European middle ages, in classical Greece, in China and Japan, and in ancient Egypt. Yet this development of interest in ancient and distant countries, which the Romantics encouraged so enthusiastically, could hardly have existed had it not been underpinned by much patient scholarship carried out within the eighteenth century.

Precisely the same situation applies in the literary arts. There were poets, such as Wordsworth, who rejected much eighteenth-century verse, on the grounds that it was conventional and routine, and who sought to revive interest in older kinds of poetry. Once again, however, the groundwork, without which such interest could not have been revived, had already been laid: *The Reliques of Ancient English Poetry*, edited by Thomas Percy (1729–1811), came out in 1765 and is only one of several similar works that might here be cited.

With such thoughts in their minds many scholars have come to the conclusion that, if Romanticism is analysed into its component features (interest in primitive man, in primitive states of society, and in primitive verse, for example) and if the history of the growth of interest in these individual features is traced, Romanticism itself seems to disappear amid the complexities of its own prehistory.

Though there are benefits to be gained from stressing how complex and elusive Romanticism is, a cruder account has benefits too. Such an account might run as follows. The Romantic poet reacts against the poetry of his immediate predecessors, probably because he thinks that it was produced in accordance with rules that restrict a poet's freedom. His reaction takes the form of an insistence that the poet should be free ('liberty' is a Romantic key-word) to treat the themes which he thinks proper in a language which he thinks appropriate. Poetry, he might well insist, is not prose that rhymes (a contemptuous dismissal of eighteenth-century verse) but instead answers human needs which prose hardly recognises and cannot satisfy. Verse alone is the proper literary medium for impassioned utterance, and the poet speaks truths of passion which, because they have no prose equivalents, are not reducible to prose without serious loss.

The Romantic belief that the poet should reacquaint us with truths about ourselves that the passionless verse of the eighteenth century had neglected was widespread. There came into being, for instance, in the 1770s a cult of 'sensibility' which maintained that people should develop their powers of feeling and rely more heavily upon truths to which feeling granted them access. The Romantics, who were influenced by this cult and who took over and intensified it, certainly stressed the value of the intensity with which a man felt his convictions. At the corrupt modern end of Romanticism this yields us D.H. Lawrence (1885-1930), pressing his hands to his solar plexus and saying, 'I don't feel it here.' But that insistence, though frequently put to better use, was within Romanticism from the start. 'Does a firm persuasion that a thing is so, make it so?' William Blake (1757-1827) asks Isaiah in a famous piece of fantasy-writing called *The Marriage of Heaven and Hell* (1790): 'He replied: "All poets believe that it does, and in ages of imagination this firm persuasion removed mountains".'

'All good poetry,' Wordsworth claimed in a famous passage in the Preface to *Lyrical Ballads*, 'is the spontaneous overflow of powerful feelings.' 'Passion' is another word for 'powerful feelings', and the truth which is the object of poetry, he added, is not to be found 'standing upon external testimony, but [is] carried alive into the heart by passion'. One of the 'characteristics of Mr Wordsworth's muse', according to Lord Byron (1788-1824), who was reviewing the 1807 poems but with *Lyrical Ballads* in mind, was 'its strong, and sometimes irresistible appeals to the feelings'.

Because the Romantic poets were in revolt against their eighteenth-century predecessors, and lived through a time of great political upheaval, they sometimes acquired the reputation of being themselves 'revolutionaries' in a wider sense of the term. Some of them, most notably Lord Byron and Percy Bysshe Shelley (1792-1822), courted this reputation eagerly and lived in open defiance of the received moral wisdom. Wordsworth, by contrast, was much more conventionally proper: his affair with Annette Vallon, which would have damaged him in the eyes of his Victorian admirers, was not public knowledge. He was also one of only very few English Romantic poets to have lived into old age, to have acquired a large family, and to have supported his wife and children through his own efforts.

Thus he presented, in later life, the image of an eminent and successful head of a family. This image was especially appealing to the Victorians who, in reaction to what they thought were the excesses of an earlier period, were busy re-emphasising the dignity and responsibility of fatherhood. Wordsworth's increasing conservatism, his 'natural piety', and his presenting himself in his poems as a teacher, also appealed to the Victorians, who stressed the value of domestic harmony, of religious earnestness, and of whatever could be shown to be instructive or improving.

A powerful explanation of why Wordsworth was so much revered as the nineteenth century progressed is the ease with which the connections between Romantic poetry and Victorian piety can be illustrated by means of reference to what he wrote. For example, that love of wild and rugged scenery, which is so much a feature of romanticism, did not discourage writers of a conventionally pious cast of mind from pointing out that the love of God and the love of a stiff climb were not incompatible. Thus the anonymous author of *The Ascent of Scawfell Pike: or a Day in the Mountains* (1851) wrote that 'When the foot is active, the frame healthy, the heart toned to nature, and the spirit grateful, a pleasant thing it is to a Christian tourist to spend a day on the mountains.'

The Victorians also laid heavy emphasis upon the value of the family, the home, and upon domestic morality and probity. (One Victorian lady, after watching Shakespeare's *Antony and Cleopatra*, is reported to have exclaimed: 'How different, how very different, from the home-life of our own dear Queen.') More than thirty years before Victoria ascended the throne, however, Wordsworth had claimed, in a letter to Charles James Fox (see below, p. 29), that in 'Michael' and 'The Brothers' he had attempted 'to draw a picture of the domestic affections as I know they exist amongst a class of men who are now almost confined to the North of England'.

The word 'domestic' really matters when we come to study Wordsworth's poetry. It derives from the Latin word *domus*, a home, and 'homes' play a peculiarly large part in Wordsworth's poetry, as a consequence, no doubt, of the unsettled home-life of his early years. 'What dwelling shall receive me?':

> In what vale
> Shall be my harbour? Underneath what grove
> Shall I take up my home?

he asks at the beginning of the first book of *The Prelude*. That early, not entirely successful poem 'The Female Vagrant' is best when it registers (1) dispossession, (2) the restorative powers of settled domestic life, or (3) the devastating contrast between having and not having a home:

(1) All, all was seized, and weeping, side by side,
     We sought a home where we uninjured might abide.

(2)   upon his neck I wept,
     And her whom he had loved in joy, he said
     He well could love in grief: his faith he kept;
     And in a quiet home once more my father slept.

(3) And homeless near a thousand homes I stood,
     And near a thousand tables pined and wanted food.

Just as 'natural piety' ('And I could wish my days to be/ Bound each to each by natural piety') can easily become 'piety', and the Religion of Nature take on the nature of religion ('I, so long/ A worshipper of Nature, hither came/ Unwearied in that service'), so domesticity (what the Female Vagrant calls 'sweet thoughts of home') can easily be converted into the orthodox social preference of the Victorian period. There was, for example, a book published in 1848 under the title of *Domestic Memoirs of a Christian Family resident in the County of Cumberland: With Descriptive Sketches of the Scenery of the English Lakes*, the profits of which were to be devoted 'to the cause, and in aid of the funds of the Church Missionary Society'. There could hardly be a neater example of how Romanticism ('Scenery of the English Lakes') and Victorianism ('Domestic Memoirs of a Christian Family') met and married: in the opinion of many latter-day observers the priest at their wedding was William Wordsworth.

A note on the text

The detailed notes which follow are linked to *Selections from Wordsworth: Poetry and Prose*, edited by Ifor Evans, Methuen, London, 1935; eleventh edition, 1966. This selection, widely used in schools and readily available, contains a large number of poems, including the first two books of *The Prelude* (1850), representative of Wordsworth's achievements over many years; reprints the Preface to *Lyrical Ballads* (1802); and has its own introduction and notes.

In the following notes attention has been concentrated on those places where the need for detailed comment is greatest: on *The Prelude* and *Lyrical Ballads*, which are heavily annotated, and on *Poems* (1807) and *Sonnets*. In contrast, the extract from *The Excursion*, an example of Wordsworth's narrative at its most straightforward, and the poems which follow it in the set-text, are more lightly glossed. A few poems, which are either very simple or of only passing interest, are not glossed at all.

Part 2

Summaries
of POEMS OF WORDSWORTH

Lyrical ballads

'The Female Vagrant'

A woman tells the story of her happy childhood, its sudden end, and the many sad adventures of her adult life. Her father is thrown out of his home by a rich and callous landowner; her husband and children die as the result of war. Though some gipsies are kind to her she cannot accept their way of life. Instead she wanders alone across the countryside.

COMMENTARY: 'The Female Vagrant' provides an excellent, though extreme, example of the many revisions to which Wordsworth subjected his poems. In 1793–4 he wrote a poem called *Salisbury Plain* in which the story of the Female Vagrant first appeared. A little later (1795 onwards) he revised the poem, calling it *Adventures on Salisbury Plain*, and then, in 1798 (while compiling *Lyrical Ballads*) extracted from it the poem now known as 'The Female Vagrant'. In 1800, in the second edition, the poem was reissued with only minor alterations: for example the 'mansion proud' (line 39) became a 'stately hall' and 'birds in May' (line 67) which had been 'little' cheered themselves up and became 'gladsome' instead. The first of these revisions removes a poetical inversion by restoring normal English word order (adjective, noun) but the second is surely a good example of Wordsworth's altering his texts without improving them.

Much greater revisions were being planned, and were first unveiled in a letter which Wordsworth wrote to a friend in 1801:

> You flatter me . . . that my style is distinguished by a genuine simplicity. Whatever merit I may have in this way I have attained solely by endeavouring to look, as I have said in my preface, steadily at my subject. If you read over carefully the Poem of the Female Vagrant, which was the first written of the Collection (indeed it was written several years before the others) you will see that I have not formerly been conscious of the importance of this rule. The diction of that Poem is often vicious, and the descriptions are often false, giving proofs of a mind inattentive to the true nature of the subject on which it was employed.

In line with these comments this poem, in the third edition of *Lyrical*

Ballads (1802), was massively revised. Hardly a stanza escaped change, and the first, third, fourth, and fourteenth were omitted altogether (though the third and fourth reappeared in 1820). Doubtless these omissions were in part designed to remove particular examples of vicious diction (look, for instance, at the third stanza) but they also reflect the early stages of Wordsworth's change of political heart.

As originally conceived *Salisbury Plain* was a poem of social protest: of protest which was gradually moderated until eventually it was entirely extinguished. The removal of the fourteenth stanza (beginning 'Oh! dreadful price of being to resign') is simply an early example of this development, but is of interest because it shows Wordsworth excluding a line that is especially characteristic of him. Consider how that stanza ends:

> . . . in the streets and walks where proud men are,
> Better our dying bodies to obtrude,
> Than dog-like, wading at the heels of war,
> Protract a curst existence, with the brood
> That lap (their very nourishment) their brother's blood.

Perhaps we do not think this very remarkable, but we need to remember that, for Wordsworth, the fraternal relationship was one of the most sacred and satisfying that life afforded. One of his most moving poems is called 'The Brothers', and the priority which he granted to the relationship between siblings is reflected in a curious turn of phrase in 'The Female Vagrant' itself. 'There was a youth,' she tells us, 'whom I had loved so long,/ That when I loved him not I cannot say':

> We talked of marriage and our marriage day;
> And I in truth did love him like a brother

We are so used to romantic novelettes, films, and serials in which the heroine tells her rejected suitor that she will always 'love him like a brother' that we are in danger of slighting the quite different feeling that Wordsworth's lines are meant to communicate. And the playing off of that feeling against the image with which the fourteenth stanza closes is one of the excellences within the poem that Wordsworth's political development led him to sacrifice.

The poem escaped alteration in 1805, but when it appeared in the two-volume *Poems, including Lyrical Ballads* (1815) it had been shorn of its first 130 lines. In 1820 these were restored. Finally, in 1840, Wordsworth returned to his original manuscripts of the poem, left on one side for nearly half a century, revised them, and had the poem, complete at last, published in 1842, under the title *Guilt and Sorrow*. So complicated is this history of pre- and post-publication change that the 1793-4, 1795-9, and 1841 manuscripts were not published in their entirety until 1975 (in the edition edited by Stephen Gill, listed in Part 5 of these Notes, 'Suggestions for further reading').

NOTES AND GLOSSARY:

By Derwent's side: Derwentwater, one of the most famous lakes in the Lake District, surrounded by some of the district's most famous mountains. Wordsworth described it thus in his *A Guide through the District of the Lakes*: 'Derwent is distinguished from all the other Lakes by being *surrounded* with sublimity: the fantastic mountains of Borrowdale to the south, the solitary majesty of Skiddaw to the north, the bold steeps of Wallow-crag and Lodore to the east, and to the west the clustering mountains of New-lands'

what the neighbouring flood/ Supplied: an elaborate way of saying that the Female Vagrant's father caught fish. A Victorian guide-book confirms that Derwentwater 'abounds with trout, perch, pike, and eel'

fleecy store: sheep (poetic diction)

The cowslip-gathering at May's dewy prime: 'prime' is one of the ancient monastic offices, sung at 6 a.m. The Female Vagrant gathers cowslips while the dew is upon them, in order, perhaps, to make cowslip wine

His little range of water was denied: his right to fish in Derwentwater (which was parcelled out among the owners of various nearby properties) was curtailed

to ply the artist's trade: the young man's father insists that he seek employment as a craftsman. 'Artist' here means 'craftsman', an older meaning of the word

daily bread: a reference to one of the petitions of the Lord's Prayer: 'Give us this day our daily bread'

equinoctial deep: twice during the year, once in March and once in September, the sun crosses the equator and day and night are of equal duration (hence 'equinox'). Because it has been delayed the Female Vagrant's ship runs into the storms associated with the September equinox

pined: languished. There was probably in Wordsworth's mind an unconscious association between this word and 'tables' (via the name of the tree). There is a similar association in Book 1 of *The Prelude* in the lines (514–17): 'Or round the naked table, snow-white deal,/ Cherry or maple, sate in close array,/ And to the combat, Loo or Whist, led on/ A thick-

	ribbed army', where 'deal', the name of a kind of wood, has suggested the action of dealing cards
the wild brood:	gipsies, who are called 'vagrants' by Wordsworth because of the wandering life they lead. It was fashionable to include them in Romantic landscape paintings and in their literary equivalents. Wordsworth calls the gipsies 'tenants' in order to distinguish them from landowners. Note, especially, the contrast between the 'master' of the fifth stanza who did not care to 'stray/ Through pastures not his own' and the gipsies, among whom 'all belonged to all, and each was chief'
the black disguise:	the blacking of the face in order to commit theft was itself a serious offence in the eighteenth century

'To my Sister'

Wordsworth tells Dorothy not to waste her time in reading, but to join him outside where there is more to be learned.

COMMENTARY: This poem was written in early March 1798 at Alfoxden, and was originally entitled 'Lines written at a small distance from my House, and sent by my little Boy to the Person to whom they are addressed'. The 'little Boy' (called Edward in the poem) was Basil Caroline Montagu (1792–1830). His father, also called Basil Montagu, was a widower, and the Wordsworths looked after his son from 1795 to 1798.

NOTES AND GLOSSARY:
There is a blessing: compare the opening of *The Prelude*

'Expostulation and Reply' and 'The Tables Turned'

In these poems Wordsworth and a friend disagree about the value of book-learning. In the first poem the friend wants Wordsworth to study more carefully. In the second Wordsworth replies that studying the natural world is better than studying books.

COMMENTARY: Both of these poems were composed at Alfoxden in late May or early June 1798. 'The lines entitled Expostulation and Reply,' Wordsworth noted in his 1798 Advertisement, 'and those which follow, arose out of conversation with a friend who was somewhat unreasonably attached to modern books of moral philosophy.' This friend is generally thought to be William Hazlitt (1778–1830), who visited Wordsworth in May 1798.

NOTES AND GLOSSARY:

else: who would otherwise be

Esthwaite lake: Hawkshead, where Wordsworth went to school, stands close to this lake. Wordsworth is taking us back to his schooldays

Matthew: in a poem entitled 'The Two April Mornings' Wordsworth refers to Matthew as 'a village school-master . . . With hair of glittering grey'. In consequence, William Taylor, the Hawkshead school-master, has sometimes been thought to be Matthew. In a late note Wordsworth warned readers not to identify Matthew too closely with any one person, since he was, he said, 'made up of several both of his class and men of other occupations'. The change of name was probably intended to discourage over-precise (and, therefore, imprecise) identification: besides, if William Wordsworth (line 1) was trans-ferring to William Taylor the opinions voiced by William Hazlitt he may well have thought some change of name convenient. The name of a friend, William Mathews, probably suggested what that change should be

---

'The Complaint of a Forsaken Indian Woman'

An Indian woman who is too weak to keep up with the rest of her tribe is left behind and her child is taken from her. She bewails her condition and longs to be reunited with her child.

COMMENTARY: This poem is believed to have been written at Alfoxden in March or early May 1798. Some of its details were derived from Samuel Hearne's *A Journey from Prince of Wales's Fort in Hudson's Bay to Northern Ocean* (1795), a book which was found in Wordsworth's library after his death. The only modern works that he read, Words-worth admitted in a letter in 1812, were 'those of travels, or such as relate to Matters of fact'.

NOTES AND GLOSSARY:

something: (line 36) this word was changed, in 1815, to 'working'

little: (line 40) this word was changed, in 1815, to 'help-less', probably to avoid undue repetition of the word, which occurs twice in the next line

My journey will be shortly run: this final stanza was omitted in 1815, but was restored, though with alterations, in 1836. Line

61 was changed to: 'Young as I am, my course is run', and lines 69–70 to:

But thou, dear Babe, art far away
Nor shall I see another day.

Since the original reading is drawn much more nearly from 'a selection of language really used by men' than that by which it is replaced, this latter change is especially worthy of note

My poor forsaken child: a good example of Wordsworth's following, in the words of his Preface, 'the fluxes and refluxes of the mind when agitated by the great and simple affections of our nature'. Though, as the title makes clear, it is the Indian Woman who is forsaken, nevertheless, even in extremity, it is of the child's loss that she thinks

---

'Lines Written a Few Miles Above Tintern Abbey'

The poet revisits a landscape which he last saw five years previously. He considers how much the landscape has influenced him, and decides that since his last visit he has grown more mature and has acquired a deeper understanding of humanity.

COMMENTARY: The inspiration that produced this poem belonged, Wordsworth claimed late in life, to 1793 when, after crossing Salisbury Plain (and thinking of the story of the Female Vagrant), he passed into Bath and Bristol and then travelled northwards, and alone, to view the picturesque scenery of the River Wye. He revisited the river, accompanied by Dorothy, in July 1798 (hence 'Five years have passed'), composed much of 'Tintern Abbey' (but without writing any of it down) while returning by boat to Bristol, composed the remainder while walking into the city, and then wrote down the completed poem immediately upon his reaching a desk and paper. The date given in the poem's title, 13 July, is that of its completion: 'July 15', in Professor Evans's edition, is a misprint.

NOTES AND GLOSSARY:

five summers, with the length/ Of five long winters!: though Wordsworth's meaning is clear, his expression of it is not beyond reproach. He does not wish to suggest that each summer was as long as a long winter

With a soft inland murmur: 'The river is not affected by the tides a few miles above Tintern' (Wordsworth's note). 'Soft' is a late reading, replacing 'sweet'

Nor, with their green and simple hue, disturb: that orchard trees, though planted by man, were not out of keeping in a natural landscape was an opinion to which Wordsworth held firmly. In *A Guide through the District of the Lakes* he told landowners who were planting shrubs near their houses that 'the various sorts of fruit-and-blossom-bearing trees usually found in orchards . . . may be happily admitted as an intermediate link between the shrubs and the forest trees'

Though absent long . . . to me: this was changed to: 'These beauteous forms,/ Through a long absence, have not been to me'. We have here a good example of one of Wordsworth's most careful revisions. Presumably he altered the earlier reading because it might suggest that it was the landscape (rather than the poet) which had been absent. The later reading lessens, though it does not altogether remove, this ambiguity

Though absent . . . life of things: Wordsworth's memory of the beautiful scenery of the River Wye has consoled and restored him while he has spent a frustrating time in towns and cities (lines 26–31). The pleasure that he experienced in 1793, though he may not have been able to recall it in detail, has by increasing his composure and balance enabled him to act with unknowing but natural kindness (lines 31–6). Finally, and the grandest gift of all, his recollection of the beauty of the Wye has helped him achieve a remarkable clarity of spiritual outlook (lines 36–50)

The picture of the mind: the picture retained by his memory, which gains new life when Wordsworth stands once again in the Wye valley

And so I dare . . . chasten and subdue: 'Tintern Abbey' in several respects parallels *The Prelude*. In that long, autobiographical poem Wordsworth tells us how his present attitude towards the world is the last of three stages through which he has passed in growing up. The first two stages are detailed in the first two books of *The Prelude*; the third is detailed in the eighth.

(a) The first stage, that of simple pleasure in living, belongs to extreme youth, and is represented in 'Tintern Abbey' by the 'coarser pleasures' and 'glad animal movements' of lines 74–5, and in *The Prelude* by the 'round of tumult' of Book II, 9.

(b) Eventually the growing boy begins to recognise that his pleasures depend, in part, upon their being acted out in appropriate weather and in pleasant surroundings. He thus attaches 'collaterally' (see *Prelude*, II, 50) some of his pleasure to the natural world, and as he grows older transfers across this attachment more and more pleasure. The gradual emergence of a love of nature from amid the chaos of childish excitements is indicated in *Prelude*, II, 131-4:

> Oh, ye rocks and streams,
> And that still spirit shed from evening air!
> Even in this joyous time I sometimes felt
> Your presence

The completion of this second stage is represented in 'Tintern Abbey' by the words 'For nature then . . . To me was all in all'. It was while Wordsworth was in this second stage of his development that he visited the Wye in 1793.

(c) The third stage grows out of the second as the second grew out of the first. Deep pleasure in the natural world carries with it, unrecognised at first, knowledge of and sympathy with the human beings who live surrounded, but not dwarfed or degraded, by the works of nature (compare 'Michael', lines 28-33). Wordsworth's most famous example of how living amid such scenery ennobles a man in the eyes of others occurs in *The Prelude*, Book 8, where he describes how a shepherd can be dignified, while striding about doing his work, by the strange effects of light and mist in mountain districts. This third stage, a love of humanity that has grown out of a love of nature, is represented in 'Tintern Abbey' by the 'still, sad music' of line 92.

Wordsworth sets out the three stages, in a manner that clearly parallels 'Tintern Abbey', in *Prelude*, VIII, 342-56. The first stage (that of early boyhood):

> Nature herself was, at this unripe time,
> But secondary to my own pursuits
> And animal activities, and all
> Their trivial pleasures . . .

leads to the second, in which nature is preeminent,

and then to the third, in which humanity comes to
the fore:

> and when these had drooped
> And gradually expired, and Nature, prized
> For her own sake, became my joy, even then—
> And upwards through late youth, until not less
> Than two-and-twenty summers had been told—
> Was Man in my affections and regards
> Subordinate to her, her visible forms
> And viewless agencies: a passion, she,
> A rapture often, and immediate love
> Ever at hand; he, only a delight
> Occasional, and accidental grace,
> His hour being not yet come.

The reading of the 1805 text of *The Prelude* ('not
less/Than three and twenty summers') links this
passage even more closely to 'Tintern Abbey'

The coarser . . . all gone by: it is generally assumed that Wordsworth's
having placed these words within parentheses indi-
cates that they are stepped back in time from the rest
of the passage in which they occur, and relate to the
first stage of his development. It is a pity that, in
describing its second stage, Wordsworth should
have employed a simile ('when like a roe/ I bounded
o'er the mountains') based upon the movement of
an animal. With 'animal movements' compare the
'animal activities' of *Prelude*, VIII, 344

Unborrowed from the eye: that is, not borrowed from the eye. Words-
worth clarifies his meaning in *Prelude*, XII, 114–21
(1850 text) where he tells us that he was at this time
guilty of: 'giving way/ To a comparison of scene
with scene,/ Bent overmuch on superficial things,/
Pampering myself with meagre novelties/ Of colour
and proportion; to the moods/ Of time and season,
to the moral power,/ The affections and the spirit of
the place,/ Insensible.'

what they half-create,/ And what perceive: 'This line has a close resemb-
lance to an admirable line of Young the exact
expression of which I cannot recollect' (Words-
worth's note). Our senses, according to Edward
Young (1683–1765) in his *Night Thoughts*, 'Take
in, at once the landscape of the world . . . And half
create the wondrous world they see'

genial spirits: spirits that were with him from his birth
Nor greetings where no kindness is: compare 'The Female Vagrant' (line
204); 'looks where common kindness had no part'
A worshipper of Nature: in 1815 Wordsworth complained of a woman
who had thoroughly misunderstood his poetry:
'She talks of my being a worshipper of Nature—a
passionate expression uttered incautiously in the
Poem upon the Wye has led her into this mistake,
she reading in cold-heartedness and substituting
the letter for the spirit'

'Strange fits of passion'

The poet explains that once, when approaching Lucy's house, he had
a premonition of her death.
COMMENTARY: This is one of the Lucy Poems, and 'a favorite of mine'
(Dorothy Wordsworth). Despite extensive research no one correspond-
ing to Lucy has ever been found; she is probably a poet's fiction, though
the poems certainly reflect Wordsworth's affection for his sister. All
of them, except 'I travell'd among unknown Men', were written in
Goslar (see The Life of William Wordsworth in Part 1 of these Notes,
p. 7) and appeared for the first time in the 1800 edition of *Lyrical
Ballads*. A letter written by William and Dorothy to Coleridge in
December 1798 provides early texts of two of the poems, and shows the
extent to which Wordsworth altered the mood of the poems when pre-
paring them for publication. See also Hints for study, in Part 4 of
these Notes.

NOTES AND GLOSSARY:
Strange fits ... to me befell: this stanza is not included in the 1798 letter
At once, the planet dropped: in 1815 'planet' was altered to 'bright
moon', a change which emphasises the appearance
of the moon in every stanza except the first and last
'If Lucy should be dead!': in the 1798 letter there is an additional stanza:
'I told her this; her laughter light/ Is ringing in my
ears;/ And when I think upon that night/ My eyes
are dim with tears.' The suppression of this stanza
and the addition of the stanza with which the poem
now opens very considerably alter its mood

'She dwelt among th' untrodden ways'

The death of Lucy, a solitary and little-known girl, affects the poet
deeply.

COMMENTARY: This was originally, in the 1798 letter, a five-stanza poem, of which the first and fourth stanzas were suppressed in the interests of greater conciseness. The original first stanza was as follows:

My hope was one, from cities far,
    Nursed on a lonesome heath;
Her lips were red as roses are,
    Her hair a woodbine wreath.

NOTES AND GLOSSARY:

springs of Dove: there are several rivers of this name in the north of England

Fair as a star: an image that may have been suggested by Lucy's name, which comes from the Latin word *lux*, light

Is shining in the sky!: this is followed in the 1798 letter by: 'And she was graceful as the broom/ That flowers by Carron's side;/ But slow distemper check'd her bloom,/ And on the Heath she died.'

She liv'd unknown . . . ceas'd to be: in the 1798 letter these lines read: Long time before her head lay low/ Dead to the world was she:/ But now she's . . .

'I travell'd among unknown men'

Having returned from a Continental visit, the poet realises that he prefers England to other countries because of its association with Lucy. COMMENTARY: This is a poem which was once thought to have been written in 1799 but which is now usually dated 1801. The sentiments, however, reflect Wordsworth's Goslar visit. In 1799, shortly after returning to England, Wordsworth wrote to a friend: 'We have spent our time pleasantly enough in Germany, but we are right glad to find ourselves in England, for we have learnt to know its value.'

NOTES AND GLOSSARY:
turn'd her wheel: a reference to the spinning-wheel

'Three years she grew in sun and shower'

Lucy is too beautiful to be allowed to live, and is reclaimed by Nature. COMMENTARY: According to Coleridge, in the twenty-second chapter of his *Biographia Literaria* (1817), the fourth of Wordsworth's great virtues was 'the perfect truth of nature in his images and descriptions, as taken immediately from nature'. He cites, as examples, the last two stanzas of 'The Green Linnet' (see below) and the whole of 'Three Years She Grew', a poem which he describes as being 'completely Wordsworth's'.

'A slumber did my spirit seal'

The poet, very conscious that Lucy is dead (lines 5–8), remembers a time when he thought that she would not die (lines 1–4).
COMMENTARY: Coleridge referred to this poem as an 'epitaph' and thought that Wordsworth was seeking to imagine the emotional consequences of his sister's death. Though that is mere speculation, the latinate 'diurnal' (daily) not only has something of the dignity of a funeral inscription but includes within itself reference to a burial urn.

'Lucy Gray or, Solitude'

Lucy Gray, sent to accompany her mother home through the snow, misses her way in a storm and is never found.
COMMENTARY: 'Lucy Gray' is not usually accounted one of the Lucy Poems despite its having been written during Wordsworth's Goslar visit, and despite obvious similarities of phrasing. The story, he claimed, was a true one that had been told him by Dorothy, and his object in writing the poem was to produce a convincing portrayal of 'entire *solitude*': hence the alternative title.

NOTES AND GLOSSARY:
Yet some maintain . . . a living Child: the body of the child was, in fact, discovered in a canal. By suppressing all mention of the discovery, Wordsworth is able to leave his ballad-like poem with a traditional haunting end

'Ruth'

Ruth; a young girl whose mother has died and whose father has remarried, meets a charming young man. She agrees to become his wife, spurred on by his exciting stories of North America, but is deserted by him and spends the rest of her days as a vagrant.
COMMENTARY: This poem, written in Germany in 1799, is one which, like 'The Forsaken Indian Woman', shows Wordsworth's indebtedness to books of travel and 'such as relate to Matters of fact'. In this instance he used a book by William Bartram, entitled *Travels through North and South Carolina* (1791).
   'Ruth' was much revised, and in 1802 seven stanzas were added after line 54.

NOTES AND GLOSSARY:
Casque: a helmet. The Cherokees (line 16) are a tribe of North American Indians

when America was free: the American War of Independence, to which reference is here made, ended in 1783

Magnolia: *Magnolia grandiflora* (Wordsworth's note); a vivid flowering shrub

Of flowers that with one scarlet gleam: 'The splendid appearance of these scarlet flowers, which are scattered with such profusion over the Hills in the Southern parts of North America is frequently mentioned by Bartram in his Travels' (Wordsworth's note)

Savannahs: grasslands, sparsely dotted with trees

a Father's love: the young man is either lucky or a shrewd seducer. Ruth, the 'slighted Child' whose 'Father took another Mate', is unlikely to resist the vision of having for her own children what she did not have herself. That the youth's original intentions are not cynical is suggested by lines 151–6

sylvan Huntress: a reference to Diana, the virgin huntress of Classical mythology. On a famous occasion she changed a man, Actaeon, into a stag, and hunted him to his death. Both as a virgin and as a huntress Ruth is less successful

at midnight shed: 'shed' here has unfortunately been caught from line 87, in which the word 'night' also appears

The wind ... workings of the heart: in a letter to John Wilson, an early admirer of his verse, Wordsworth wrote that 'there cannot be a doubt that in tracts of country where images of danger, melancholy, grandeur, or loveliness, softness, and ease prevail, that they will make themselves felt powerfully in forming the characters of the people, so as to produce a uniformity of national character, where the nation is small and is not made up of men who, inhabiting different soils, climates, &c by their civil usages, and relations materially interfere with each other' (7 June 1802)

'God help thee, Ruth!': the narrator's compassionate prayer is appropriate. 'Ruth', as well as being a woman's name (biblical in origin), is also a word that means 'pity', or 'compassion', or 'regret'. The verb 'rue' and the adjective 'ruthless' are still fairly commonly used. Compare 'The Female Vagrant' (lines 258–9): 'But, what afflicts my peace with keenest ruth/ Is, that I have my inner self abused'

the pleasant banks of Tone: 'The Tone is a River of Somersetshire at no great distance from the Quantock Hills. These

Hills, which are alluded to a few stanzas below, are extremely beautiful, and in most places richly covered with Coppice woods' (Wordsworth's note)

Under the greenwood tree: traditionally the meeting place of lovers. Wordsworth's use of the phrase is deliberately ironical

And other home hath none: contrast this with the young man's promise (line 72) that Ruth will find 'a home in every glade'

hallow'd mould: consecrated ground

'The Fountain'

An old man, though normally cheerful, gives himself over to sorrowful reflections, and tells a young boy of the disadvantages of old age. (For a discussion of Matthew's identity see the notes on 'Expostulation and Reply', p. 17.)

NOTES AND GLOSSARY:

Catch: an elaborate and often humorous musical composition; a sort of musical tongue-twister

'Thus fares it still ... enough belov'd': Coleridge claims in his *Biographia Literaria* that of Wordsworth's shorter poems 'there is scarcely one, which is not rendered valuable by some just and original reflection'. He picks out these six stanzas for special praise

---

'Michael'

In order to prevent his land from falling into a stranger's grip, Michael, an old man who has married late in life, sends his young son to work in the city. There the boy falls into bad company and brings disgrace upon himself and his family. The land is lost, and Michael's hopes are dashed, but his sad story lives on after his death.

COMMENTARY: The origins of the poem are to be found in Wordsworth's desire to say something memorable about the sort of life that he valued and which he thought was disappearing; and, also, in his need to make up pages in the second edition of *Lyrical Ballads*. The first edition, despite Wordsworth's fears and his later claims to the contrary, was moderately well received, and he was thus able to press on happily with his greatly expanded second edition. There was, however, one problem: 'The Rime of the Ancyent Marinere' (its title in 1798) was not well thought of, and Wordsworth feared that its prominent place as first poem in the volume had discouraged prospective buyers. Also, since the first edition contained no indication of dual authorship, he may have feared that readers would have thought that the poem was his. (A brief sketch of the early history of *Lyrical Ballads* appears in Part 3 of these notes.)

This second edition came out in January 1801, though the title-page, for reasons which are explained below, is dated 1800. It was a two-volume work, the second volume of which consisted of poems that had not previously been published. The first volume in effect reproduced the single volume of 1798, though there were significant changes. Wordsworth's authorship was acknowledged on the title-page: Coleridge's was not, neither there nor anywhere else in the two volumes. But he was referred to as 'a Friend', and the poems that he had written were acknowledged not to be by Wordsworth. The 'Ancient Mariner', already considerably revised, was moved so as to become the penultimate poem in the first volume (it preceded 'Tintern Abbey'). In an insensitive note Wordsworth laid bare its chief failings, as he saw them, while allowing it to have 'a value which is not often possessed by better Poems'.

Nevertheless, despite this slighting of the 'Ancient Mariner', it was intended that Coleridge should contribute to the second volume. He set to work and produced 'Christabel', with which, on 4 October 1800, Dorothy Wordsworth noted that she was 'exceedingly delighted'. On the next day she further noted that 'Coleridge read a 2nd time *Christabel*; we had increasing pleasure.' On 6 October, however, she added that it had been decided (she does not say by whom) that 'Christabel' should not form part of *Lyrical Ballads*, perhaps, though this is something of a mystery, because Wordsworth and Coleridge thought of issuing the poem separately on some other occasion and in the company of other poems. (The serious student should certainly read both the 'Ancient Mariner' and 'Christabel'.)

Whatever the reason for not including 'Christabel', its exclusion left Wordsworth with a very great problem: 'It is my wish and determination,' he wrote to his printer, 'that (whatever the expence may be, which I hereby take upon myself) such Pages of the Poem of Christabel as have been printed (if any such there be) be cancelled—I mean to have other poems substituted.' He then set about the task of making good the cancellation with all of his customary resolve. 'After dinner,' Dorothy wrote in her journal (11 October 1800), 'we walked up Greenhead Gill in search of a sheepfold.'

There then followed, dotted throughout the entries for the next few weeks, references to Wordsworth's slow progress in writing his poem, slow progress that must have been especially galling in view of the fact that his printer needed copy quickly ('you may *now* and henceforth *depend* on being supplied without any intermissions,' Wordsworth had promised him when he cancelled 'Christabel'). These entries speak for themselves: 'William again composed at the sheep-fold after dinner' (15 October); 'William worked all the morning at the sheepfold, but in vain' (18 October); 'William worked in the morning at the sheepfold' (20 October); 'William composed without much success at the sheep-fold' (22 October). Most interesting of all is the entry for 11 November 1800: 'William had been working at the sheepfold. They were salving sheep.' This last reference confirms that in these entries Dorothy is not only telling us which poem Wordsworth was composing but also where he was composing it. Accordingly, we can perhaps see some of the poet's own weariness as the poem proved stubborn in the much admired lines in which we are told of Michael that:

> 'tis believ'd by all
> That many and many a day he thither went,
> And never lifted up a single stone.

Nevertheless, despite the ill omens (the original Michael had lived in Dove Cottage), the poem did not suffer the fate of the sheepfold. On 9 December 1800 it was finished and was then hurried off to the printer. As a result the second edition of *Lyrical Ballads* was able to appear, slightly later than originally planned, in January 1801.

'Each of these poems has a purpose', Wordsworth claimed in his Preface to *Lyrical Ballads*. What purpose did he have in mind when he wrote 'Michael'? The answer is contained in a letter sent to a friend in April 1801. In 'Michael', Wordsworth wrote:

> I have attempted to give a picture of a man, of strong mind and lively sensibility, agitated by two of the most powerful affections of the human heart; the parental affection, and the love of property, *landed* property, including the feelings of inheritance, home, and personal and family independence.

Few poets can have written more helpful glosses upon their own work, in words of more commanding clarity. Wordsworth, in 'Michael', is writing in defence of the owners of small properties, and he values 'ownership' because owning things confers independence and a sense of belonging: Michael belongs to the land which belongs to him. Wordsworth is not, we should note, portraying in all its evil a man who puts property above family (as some readers of the poem have supposed). The family, ideally considered, is a group of people living on, and being buried near, land which they have long owned. Thus parental love and the 'love of property, *landed* property' are both genuine, powerful affections, intimately connected with each other: one should own the land upon which one's children are born, and which will pass to them upon one's death. But in 'Michael' we are shown the sad consequences of having these affections set in opposition to each other.

Michael knows what the risks are in sending Luke to the city, and more
than half knows that his son will fail. When Isabel lay by Michael's side:

> she for the last two nights
> Heard him, how he was troubled in his sleep:
> And when they rose at morning she could see
> That all his hopes were gone.

Yet Luke is not a victim of his father's covetousness, for the prize upon
which Michael's eyes are set is one which demands, and which is worth,
any amount of risk.

The deep feeling with which 'Michael' was written is suggested in
another of Wordsworth's letters, addressed this time to Charles James
Fox. In 'Michael', Wordsworth informed Fox:

> I have attempted to draw a picture of the domestic affections as I
> know they exist amongst a class of men who are now almost confined
> to the North of England. They are small independent *proprietors* of
> land . . . The domestic affections will always be strong amongst men
> who live in a country not crowded with population, if these men are
> placed above poverty. But if they are proprietors of small estates,
> which have descended to them from their ancestors, the power which
> these affections will acquire amongst such men is inconceivable by
> those who have only had an opportunity of observing hired labourers,
> farmers, and the manufacturing Poor. *Their little tract of land serves*
> *as a kind of permanent rallying point for their domestic feelings*
> [present author's italics] . . . This class of men is rapidly disappearing.

It is his sadness at the disappearance of this class of men and at the
destruction of their way of life that Wordsworth records with such
spare but genuine feeling in this poem.

NOTES AND GLOSSARY:

A Pastoral Poem: (*subtitle*) 'Michael' is a pastoral poem because it is
one of 'those tales that spake to me/ Of Shepherds'.
By using the term Wordsworth calls to mind, and
then rejects, those highly conventionalised pastoral
poems that are filled with references to classical
shepherds and shepherdesses with such names as
Tityrus or Amaryllis

Green-head Gill: a gill (Wordsworth sometimes uses the spelling
'ghyll') is a narrow mountain stream, often wooded.
Greenhead Gill is about a mile north-west of Dove
Cottage

a straggling heap: 'The sheepfold is falling away. It is built nearly in
the form of a heart unequally divided' (Dorothy

Wordsworth's journal, 11 October 1800). Dorothy's choice of phrase may help explain the frequent and powerful occurrence of the word 'heart' in this poem

a story entertains: late in his life Wordsworth explained that the story of Luke was based on that of a family who had once owned Dove Cottage

even more/ Than his own Blood: in 1832 Wordsworth altered this passage so that it read: 'Those fields, those hills— what could they less? had laid/ Strong hold on his affections, were to him/ A pleasurable feeling of blind love,/ The pleasure which there is in life itself.' Probably he wanted to rid himself of the ambiguity in the words 'even more/ Than his own Blood'. Yet it is the presence of this ambiguity which makes the original reading good, and its absence which impoverishes the 1832 revision. When the reader first comes across the words, before being told of either Isabel or Luke, 'Blood' (even with its capital initial) refers simply to the blood in Michael's veins. Later on, it becomes clear that Luke, too, is Michael's blood, blood which Michael is prepared to hazard in efforts to save his property

stirring: busy, active

telling: counting

card: comb

the village near the Lake: Grasmere

Evening Star: though, as explained above, Dove Cottage was the home of the original Michael and Luke, it was another cottage 'on the same side of the valley more to the north' that was known as the Evening Star

The Clipping Tree: called such because in its shade the sheep were clipped or sheared

coppice: a small wood that is regularly cut so as to produce new growth, suitable for making sticks or for weaving into hurdles

patrimonial: 'patrimony' is property that is passed down from father to son. Michael has inherited the land from his father. If he sells it he will be unable to pass it on to Luke, and the patrimony will be broken

into a Stranger's hand: one of several lines in the earlier part of 'Michael' that are repeated later (compare line 485). Compare also lines 39–45 of 'The Female Vagrant'

Richard Bateman: Robert Bateman ('Richard' is Wordsworth's mis-

take) rebuilt a chapel between Kendal and Amble-
side in 1743

Parish-boy: an orphan, or other poor boy, supported out of parish funds. (Such funds had to be made available to those in need provided that they had been born within the parish boundaries)

close to the brook side: 'A sheepfold . . . is an unroofed building of stone walls, with different divisions . . . generally placed by the side of a brook, for the convenience of washing the sheep' (Wordsworth)

My Son,/ Tomorrow thou wilt leave me . . .: Michael's impressive and spare manner of speaking is Wordsworth's way of suggesting that he merits comparison with the shepherd-patriarchs of the Old Testament. The suggestion was not his alone; a contemporary traveller wrote of the people of the Lake District that: 'removed by their situation and circumstances from the ever-shifting scene of fashionable life, their manners continue primitive . . . their hospitality is unbounded and sincere; their sentiments simple; and their language scriptural'. The same traveller mentions one shepherd who said 'I know him not; but he will receive you kindly, for our sheep mingle upon the mountains'

Wrought: worked

Meantime Luke began . . . beyond the seas: the summary depiction of metropolitan vice, and the opposing of it to Lake District virtue, is the weakest part of the poem. Admittedly it is Michael, not his son, who is at the poem's centre of interest, but it is nevertheless difficult to excuse the way in which Luke is hurried out of both poem and country. 'At length' (line 453) has no force at all

Would break the heart: for a discussion of 'heart', one of Wordsworth's key-words, see the answer to the question 'Is Wordsworth a Nature poet?' in Part 3 of these notes

That many and many . . . a single stone: Wordsworth's meaning is that Michael on many of the occasions when he visited the sheepfold did not lift up a stone. He does not mean that he did nothing every time that he visited it

Poems, 1807 (1802–7)

'To the Cuckoo'

The poet, listening to the song of the cuckoo, is reminded of former days. COMMENTARY: When Wordsworth issued his *Collected Poems* in 1815, 'To the Cuckoo' was included in a section entitled 'Poems of the Imagination'. In a preface Wordsworth pointed out that the word 'imagination', as used in that section heading, had 'no reference to images that are merely a faithful copy, existing in the mind, of absent external objects' but, instead, was 'a word of higher import, denoting operations of the mind upon those objects'. (Compare 'Tintern Abbey', where he writes of 'all the mighty world/ Of eye, and ear, both what they *half create,*/ And what perceive'.) He is not, he is insisting, merely a descriptive poet (for description 'supposes all the higher qualities of the mind to be passive') but is one who tries to show how our minds grasp, and develop, and display what our experience presents to us. In helping to explain his meaning he provides the gloss that is reproduced below.

NOTES AND GLOSSARY:

O Cuckoo! . . . a Wandering Voice: 'This concise interrogation characterises the seeming ubiquity of the voice of the cuckoo, and dispossesses the creature almost of a corporeal existence; the Imagination being tempted to this exertion of her power by a consciousness in the memory that the cuckoo is almost perpetually heard throughout the season of spring, but seldom becomes an object of sight.' The poet hears the cuckoo's song wherever he turns, but never sees the bird; he therefore, supposes, by an exercise of the imagination, that the bird is a bodiless voice (a known impossibility)

'Resolution and Independence'

The poet is unaccountably saddened, but, in wandering across a moor, meets an old man who makes a poor living by gathering leeches. Despite the nature of his work, and the precariousness of his life, the old man has not had his spirit crushed. The poet is revived by their meeting. COMMENTARY: This is the only poem in the 1807 volumes that seriously challenges comparison with the narrative poems of *Lyrical Ballads*, a point recognised by Wordsworth when in 'Poems of the Imagination' he had it printed immediately after 'Ruth' and before 'The Thorn'. In response to adverse criticism, especially that of Coleridge, Wordsworth altered the text of this poem, but it is the first published version which Evans prints and which is here glossed. The inspiration for the poem lay in a meeting with a leech-gatherer in October 1800 (recorded in Dorothy's journal).

NOTES AND GLOSSARY:

the Stock-dove broods: Wordsworth's note on this line in the 1815 preface (see 'To the Cuckoo') is difficult but illuminating: 'The stock-dove is said to *coo*, a sound well imitating the note of the bird; but, by the intervention of the metaphor *broods*, the affections are called in by the imagination to assist in marking the manner in which the bird reiterates and prolongs her soft note, as if herself delighting to listen to it, and participating of a still and quiet satisfaction, like that which may be supposed inseparable from the continuous process of incubation.' Wordsworth is once again seeking to distinguish between the poet and the man who merely describes the world. The latter's choice of word ('coos') is an excellent imitation of the sound of the bird but fails to indicate how the poet reacts to it. He (if he is Wordsworth) may decide that the care with which the dove apparently tends and contemplates its song, and derives satisfaction from it, is best conveyed by suggesting that the bird treats its song as though it were a clutch of eggs that it wishes to hatch, and so 'broods' over it

But, as it . . . nor could name: in an excellent account of the poem, included in a letter, Wordsworth provides the following note on this stanza: 'I describe myself as having been exalted to the highest pitch of delight by the joyousness and beauty of Nature and then as depressed, even in the midst of those beautiful objects, to the lowest dejection and despair' (14 June 1802). The woman to whom the letter was addressed was Sara Hutchinson, who, shortly afterwards, became Wordsworth's sister-in-law

He: the poet

Chatterton: Thomas Chatterton (1752–70), a poet of unusual precocity, who died by his own hand in despair and destitution

Him who walk'd: Robert Burns (1759–96)

Now, whether . . . wore grey hairs: in the letter to Sara, Wordsworth discusses an early (now lost) version of this stanza that must have been even more impressive than the one which survives: 'A person reading this Poem with feelings like mine will have been awed and controuled, expecting almost something spiritual and supernatural—What is brought forward? "A lonely place, a Pond" "by which an old man *was*, far from all house or home"—not stood, not sat, but "*was*"—the figure presented in the most naked simplicity possible'

As a huge stone: in 1815 Wordsworth singled out this line and the image which it inaugurates for special comment. The old man is like a rock: but that simile, though it does justice to his lack of movement, is false because he is not inanimate. The truth is that he is like an animated rock, 'a thing endued with sense'. By means of a further image, in which the rock is said to be 'like a sea-beast', what was excellent in the original image is preserved, what was defective is amended, and the result is that a 'just comparison' is achieved. (It would be difficult to imagine a better model of careful critical analysis than the one which Wordsworth here provides)

in Scotland use: 'He was of Scotch parents, but had been born in the army . . . He lived by begging, and was making his way to Carlisle, where he should buy a few godly books to sell' (Dorothy Wordsworth's journal, 3 October 1800)

While he was talking thus: 'You speak of his speech as tedious: everything is tedious when one does not read with the feelings of the Author—*The Thorn* is tedious to hundreds; and so is the *Idiot Boy* to hundreds. It is in the character of the old man to tell his story in a manner which an *impatient* reader must necessarily feel as tedious. But Good God! Such a figure, in such a place, a pious self-respecting, miserably infirm . . . Old Man telling such a tale!' (Wordsworth to Sara Hutchinson, 14 June 1802)

'To H.C., Six Years Old'

The poet is afraid that a painful future lies in store for a delicate and much-loved child. He comforts himself by reflecting that Nature will treat the child tenderly, either by exempting him from pain or by releasing him from life as soon as pain and suffering approach.

COMMENTARY: This poem is addressed to Hartley Coleridge (1796–1849), eldest child of Wordsworth's friend. Compare the following extract from a letter: 'Hartley is grown taller; he is still exceedingly slender, and there is so much thought and feeling in his face that it is scarcely possible for a person with any tenderness to look at him with indifference' (Dorothy Wordsworth, 20 June 1804).

'The Green Linnet'

Wordsworth, seated in his orchard, listens to the birds as they sing and watches the wind stirring the spring-time leaves. One bird, the green linnet, seems to sing for the sake of singing, not in order to mate, and sometimes looks like one of the leaves amongst which it perches. (See the notes on 'Three years she grew in sun and shower', p. 23.)

'Rob Roy's Grave'

Wordsworth visited what he thought was the grave of Rob Roy (1671–1734), the famous Scottish adventurer, in 1803. He later admitted that he had by mistake seen the wrong grave. Rob Roy takes his political philosophy not from books, which merely confuse a man, but from Nature, which tells him that it is right for those who are strong to snatch what they want and to hold on to it. (See note on line 65.)

NOTES AND GLOSSARY:

Robin Hood: the most famous of the outlaws of medieval England, popularly supposed to have lived with a band of loyal supporters in a forest in Nottinghamshire, and from there to have resisted the tyrannous incursions of Prince John and his lackeys

an age too soon: having set out Rob Roy's principle of conduct (broadly speaking, that 'might is right'), Wordsworth suggests that he suffered the misfortune of living too late, in a world where such conduct could not be successful. Wordsworth then corrects himself hurriedly, in order to argue that perhaps Rob Roy died too soon. If alive now he could carry out his principle on an international scale and become a Scottish Napoleon. But (line 97 onwards) Wordsworth then withdraws this argument and claims that Rob Roy, unlike Napoleon, would never have done anything to restrict 'the *liberty* of man'

her present Boast: Napoleon

'The Solitary Reaper'

Wordsworth sees a solitary woman cutting and binding grain, and hears her singing. He asks what is the subject matter of her song. He cannot answer his own question, but the song is one which he will long remember.

NOTES AND GLOSSARY:

Behold her . . . the sound: a reaper 'cuts and binds' the grain harvest. Dorothy Wordsworth noted that it was not uncommon in the Highlands to find a single person employed in this task. Wordsworth emphasises the reaper's solitariness: 'single in the field', 'solitary Highland Lass', 'Reaping and singing by herself', 'Alone she cuts'

Long after it was heard no more: though Wordsworth had seen reapers during his 1803 tour of Scotland he admitted that his poem was inspired by, and its last line taken directly from, a manuscript tour of Scotland made by a friend

'I wandered lonely as a cloud'

The poet describes his having seen daffodils beside a lake. In remembering the beautiful scene in future years he will recapture the pleasure with which he first viewed it.

COMMENTARY: This, the most frequently quoted of all Wordsworth's shorter poems, is heavily indebted to a passage in his sister's journal (15 April 1802).

NOTES AND GLOSSARY:

dancing: later changed to 'golden', in order to avoid a word that also occurs in line 6

Ten thousand: changed in 1815 to 'Fluttering and'. The change was needed because of the line 'Ten thousand saw I at a glance' which occurs in what is now the poem's second stanza. This second stanza was added in 1815

in sprightly dance: the daffodils 'tossed and reeled and danced, and seemed as if they verily laughed with the wind, that blew upon them over the lake' (Dorothy Wordsworth)

laughing: Henry Crabb Robinson (1775–1867), another of Wordsworth's circle of literary acquaintances,

noted in his diary in 1815 that 'he has substituted
. . . "jocund" for "laughing" applied to daffodils;
but he will probably restore the original . . . We
agreed in preferring the original reading'. 'Jocund',
however, once introduced, was never removed

They flash . . . of solitude: supplied by Mary Wordsworth. Wordsworth
thought these the best lines in the poem

'She was a phantom of delight'

In this poem Wordsworth describes his wife and his reaction to her. He
chooses to depict three points in their developing relationship: when
they first met; as they began to know each other better; and now that
they are married.

NOTES AND GLOSSARY:

machine: she is said to be a 'machine' because the several
aspects of her personality (as listed in line 26) work
together efficiently. The modern meaning of the
word as applied to a human being (one who acts
mechanically and without intelligence) is not
intended

'Ode to Duty'

Wordsworth dedicates himself afresh to Duty, having tired of a life in
which men agree to do whatever they want rather than what they ought.
The best people, however, are those whose wishes coincide with their
responsibilities.

COMMENTARY: This poem was probably written early in 1804, rather
than in 1805 (the traditional dating). In a letter to Coleridge, Words-
worth linked it with his political sonnets, 'Character of the Happy
Warrior', and 'Rob Roy's Grave', and said that they were poems
'relating to the social and civic duties' and were 'chiefly interesting to
the imagination through the understanding, and not to the under-
standing through the imagination' (5 May 1809).

NOTES AND GLOSSARY:

a Rod: a cane or stick with which children are beaten (as in
the proverb 'Spare the rod and spoil the child')

There are . . . know it not: Wordsworth here refers to people whose
natural kindness leads them to do, without asking
what is their duty, those things which duty does
indeed require of them

And bless'd are they . . . to their need: those people are blessed who
               believe it better to act out of natural kindness than
               from a sense of duty but who fall back upon the
               latter whenever the former runs thin

I, loving freedom . . . if I may: though never characterised by extreme
               fickleness (line 26), Wordsworth has nevertheless
               done what he wished to do, rather than what he
               ought

Through no . . . of thought: Wordsworth means that his request that
               duty should assume greater control over his life is a
               calm and reasoned one, not the consequence of
               emotional distress or strong internal prompting

a second Will more wise: Wordsworth later removed the stanza with
               which this line ends, perhaps because he realised
               that he had unwittingly punned upon his own name

Bondman: a servant who is not allowed to choose his employ-
               ment or change his employer

'Ode: Intimations of Immortality'

The poet is aware of a loss of vividness in his appreciation of the natural
world (I–IV). He explains the loss by supposing that there was a time,
prior to his birth, when his soul was attuned to God and in harmony
with Nature, but that the child loses this close contact as he grows older
and loses also the vividness of his response to Nature (V–VIII). Never-
theless, although adults lack the perceptiveness of children, they do not
entirely forget what they once knew. Their task is not to regret what
has passed but to rejoice that not everything has deserted them, to
build upon what remains, and to grow in sympathetic understanding
of humankind (IX–XI).

COMMENTARY: The first four stanzas of the 'Ode' (as it was originally
known; the longer title first appeared in 1815) were written in March
1802. Wordsworth continued the poem, perhaps as far as stanza VIII,
in June 1802, but did not finish it until early in 1804. In the letter to
Coleridge already mentioned (see the notes on the previous poem)
Wordsworth proposed grouping together 'poems relating to childhood,
and such feelings as rise in the mind in after life in direct contemplation
of that state'. The last poem in that group, occupying the place of
honour, was to be 'the grand ode'. He further proposed adopting the
last three lines of 'My heart leaps up' ('The Child is Father of the Man
. . .') as a motto for the poems of this group, and from 1815 onwards
placed these same three lines at the head of his 'Ode'.

NOTES AND GLOSSARY:

There was a time: 'This poem rests entirely upon two recollections of childhood, one that of a splendour in the objects of sense which is passed away, and the other an indisposition to bend to the law of death as applying to our own particular case. A Reader who has not a vivid recollection of these feelings having existed in his mind in childhood cannot understand that poem' (Wordsworth, in a letter written in 1815). Whatever it was that Wordsworth thought he had lost (the 'splendour . . . which is passed away'), he evidently did not think of himself as having been its sole possessor; his readers, too, should have a recollection of some long-faded splendour, and mourn its passing (See, further, the note on line 9)

the freshness of a dream: 'To that dream-like vividness and splendour which invest objects of sight in childhood, everyone, I believe, if he would look back, could bear testimony' (Wordsworth, discussing this poem late in his life)

of yore: in the past, formerly

I now can see no more: John Stuart Mill (1806–73), the famous Victorian philosopher and political economist, wrote in his *Autobiography* of 'the famous Ode . . . in which, along with the two passages of grand imagery but bad philosophy so often quoted, I found that he too had had similar experience to mine; that he also had felt that the first freshness of youthful enjoyment of life was not lasting; but that he had sought for compensation, and found it, in the way in which he was now teaching me to find it'. 'I needed to be made to feel,' Mill also wrote, 'that there was real, permanent happiness in tranquil contemplation. Wordsworth taught me this, not only without turning away from, but with a greatly increased interest in, the common feelings and common destiny of human beings'

tabor: a small drum

A timely utterance gave that thought relief: though most critics think that Wordsworth is here referring to one of his own poems, the identity of the poem has not been conclusively established. 'My heart leaps up' and 'Resolution and Independence' have both been proposed, but one should not entirely discard the possibility of the timely utterance's having been something that somebody said to Wordsworth

Cataracts: waterfalls

coronal: probably here a head-dress of interwoven foliage. Sometimes a golden and bejewelled circlet

pulling: changed to 'culling', a more dignified word (as befits a very dignified poem) but less vivid. Wordsworth, presumably, did not pronounce the final 'g', and the rhyme with 'sullen' is, therefore, good. (Elsewhere he rhymes 'doing' and 'ruin')

Our birth is but a sleep . . .: almost certainly the first of the two passages of 'grand imagery but bad philosophy' to which Mill drew his readers' attention

that imperial palace whence he came: the doctrine that Wordsworth has been expounding and which he sums up in this line (that of the pre-existence of the human soul) is not a Christian doctrine at all. Wordsworth was anxious to point out that he had adopted it in this poem not in order to enforce or encourage belief in it but merely because it was widely known and could serve as a mythical explanation of what he is really discussing. 'I took hold of the notion of pre-existence,' he claimed late in life, 'as having sufficient foundation in humanity for authorizing me to make for my purpose the best use of it I could as a Poet.' In the 'Ode' he takes for granted, as something that we have all shared, the superior vividness of some of our sensations in childhood, and their gradual fading as maturity approaches. This loss of vividness leads him to suggest that there is, perhaps, a time (prior to birth) when the human soul is especially sensitive and perceptive, and that we begin to lose sensitivity and perceptiveness as soon as we are born, and lose them more and more thoroughly as we grow older. But this suggested (or 'mythical') explanation of our sense of loss matters less than establishing that the sense of loss, though real, need not lead us on to despair (see line 182). The poem, as Mill recognised, offers us 'compensation'

cons another part: the allusion, in this line and the next, is to the speech in Shakespeare's *As You Like It* (II.7) in which Jacques compares man to an actor who plays in turn each of the seven roles that take him from his cradle to his grave. 'Humorous stage' is a quotation from a poem by Samuel Daniel (1562–1619)

Thou . . . as life!: this stanza is addressed to the Child

Thou best Philosopher: 'In what sense,' Coleridge asked in the *Biographia Literaria*, 'is a child of that age a *philosopher*? In what sense does he *read* "the eternal deep"? In what sense is he declared to be *"for ever haunted"* by the Supreme Being? or so inspired as to deserve the splendid titles of a *mighty prophet*, a *blessed seer*?' Unable to answer these, and a great many other questions, he concluded that Wordsworth was here guilty of '*mental* bombast'

Haunted for ever: the poem is about the loss that children suffer as they grow older: what does it mean to say of even one child that he is 'haunted *for ever* by the eternal mind'? Wordsworth may be generalising here: the Child is for ever haunted, just as the Child is for ever young, though individual children grow up and lose this vivid contact with God, or Nature (or the Supreme Being). Another possibility, though a less attractive one, is that Wordsworth means that the child reads 'the eternal deep (which is) haunted for ever by the eternal mind'

where we in waiting lie: Coleridge thought this a 'frightful notion'

dost thou provoke/ The Years to bring: the Child, as children commonly do, wishes that he were older

But for those . . . abolish or destroy!: a difficult passage, even by the standards of an admittedly difficult poem. The meaning is probably as follows: the vividness of the child's experience of the world is a result of its being a strange, unexplored place to him. He asks questions about it, and gradually, in the process of growing up, collects answers. These answers reduce its strangeness and help to lessen the vividness of his experience. But Wordsworth remembers with gratitude that time when the world was still a new place, when encountering it was an adventure and a challenge. Our still finding the world a challenge and a thing to be interested in is what we owe to those early years (when its strangeness provoked our questions) and can never be entirely wiped away

Yet: still

Another race: Wordsworth is looking back over his childhood days and decides that the challenges accepted then (in what he now sees to have been 'another race') and the victories won ('other palms') are firmly in the past, but that fresh challenges and the hope of newer victories greet the mature man

'Character of the Happy Warrior'

The poet sets out the moral qualities which characterise the ideal military gentleman: kindness, scrupulousness, openness, decency, faithfulness and bravery.

COMMENTARY: Wordsworth had Admiral Lord Nelson (1758–1805) and John Wordsworth (1771–1805) in mind when he wrote this verse-catalogue of the qualities that make a man excellent.

NOTES AND GLOSSARY:

manna: the food with which God kept alive the Israelites during their journeys in the desert (see Exodus 16)

'Lines (Composed at Grasmere)'

The valley streams, swollen by storms, seem to Wordsworth to register his distress at the impending death of the politician Charles James Fox (1749–1806), a man of more than usual sensitivity and public-spiritedness. He concludes, however, that the death of good men merely returns them to their Creator, and is not to be mourned.

Sonnets (1802–31)

Sonnets, according to Wordsworth in 1815, belong to the fourth of the six classes into which he divides poetry. Poems of this class are 'descriptive chiefly either of the processes and appearances of external nature . . . or of characters, manners, and sentiments'.

Wordsworth is seeking to distinguish such poems from narrative poems (which tell a story), from dramatic poems (in which the poet speaks in an assumed voice), from lyric poems (which he narrowly defines as those in which 'for the production of their *full* effect, an accompaniment of music is required'), and from didactic (or instructive) and satirical poems.

Like most attempts at dividing poetry into a limited number of categories, this one fails to take proper account of those poems which span its divisions. Some of Wordsworth's sonnets ('Composed upon Westminster Bridge' is a good example) fall naturally into his fourth category; many more do not.

Three of the sonnets printed by Professor Evans ('I griev'd for Buonaparté', 'Is it a reed', and 'To Toussaint L'Ouverture') were among seven that were published in the *Morning Post* in 1803 and of which an editorial justly asserted that 'each forms a little Political Essay, on some recent proceeding'. These sonnets, true to the influence upon them (which is that of Milton), are not concerned to describe 'the processes and appearances of external nature'; and they reflect upon, rather than merely reflect, 'characters, manners, and sentiments'. They are thus unashamedly instructive, as a glance at the sestet (the last six lines) of 'I griev'd for Buonaparté' will make quite clear.

John Milton (1608–74) is the most famous of those English poets who have tried to make the sonnet something more than a declaration of love or verbal representation of natural beauty. Wordsworth's admiration of Milton is evident, nowhere more strongly than in the sonnet which he addresses to him ('Milton! thou should'st be living at this hour'). That the older poet was an immediate, not merely a distant, influence is demonstrated by a telling entry in Dorothy Wordsworth's journal: 'William wrote two sonnets on Buonaparte, after I had read Milton's sonnets to him' (21 May 1802). Furthermore the influence was not a matter of content or style alone, but dictated also the form of the sonnet that Wordsworth chose to employ.

The distinctive feature of the sonnet is its length, which is always fourteen lines. The Italian or Petrarchan form, which both Milton and Wordsworth adopt, rhymes in its 'octave': *abba, abba*; and in its 'sestet': *cdcdcd* or *cdecde* or something similar. Though Wordsworth makes full use of permissible variations in rhyme scheme ('I griev'd for Buonaparté' rhymes *abba, abab, c, ddcdc*) he rarely uses more than five rhyming words and very often uses only four. By contrast the English form of the sonnet, employed by Shakespeare and firmly associated with his name, is divisible into three 'quatrains' and a concluding couplet: *abab, cdcd, efef, gg*. Whatever the merits of the two forms, the Italian Sonnet is certainly the more difficult to achieve in English. Wordsworth's attempts frequently contain redundancies ('playing by the score') and poor rhymes ('bend the knee / Majesty')—though sometimes an apparently poor rhyme is simply evidence of Wordsworth's north-country accent ('thought / not').

'I griev'd for Buonaparté'

Instead of being great warriors men who assume political control over the destinies of nations should be practised in the humbler arts of kindliness and of domestic solicitude.

COMMENTARY: Wordsworth's approval of the initial stages of the revolution in France was tempered by his disapproval of its later excesses.

The rise of Napoleon from the ranks and his assumption of supreme power were regarded by Wordsworth as the re-emergence of monarchy in a new and deadlier form.

NOTES AND GLOSSARY:

vital blood: Wordsworth later changed this to 'tenderest mood'. Presumably he feared a mixed metaphor, the mind having no blood. But the mixed metaphor, if it is one, is preferable to its bloodless replacement

---

'Composed upon Westminster Bridge'

The sleeping city, viewed in early morning sunlight, is as beautiful as a natural landscape.

COMMENTARY: In July 1802 Wordsworth and Dorothy crossed Westminster Bridge on their way to Dover, and from there to Calais, where Wordsworth wanted to talk to Annette Vallon about his impending marriage to Mary Hutchinson. Dorothy records their crossing of the bridge in words that invite comparison with her brother's poem: 'It was a beautiful morning. The city, St Paul's, with the river and a multitude of little boats, made a most beautiful sight as we crossed Westminster Bridge. The houses were not overhung by their cloud of smoke, and they were spread out endlessly, yet the sun shone so brightly, with such a fierce light, that there was even something like the purity of one of nature's own grand spectacles' (31 July 1802).

NOTES AND GLOSSARY:

like a garment: when it was pointed out to Wordsworth that he describes the city as being clothed in this line but says that it is 'bare' in the next, he replied that 'the contradiction is in the *words* only—bare, as not being covered with smoke or vapour; clothed, as being attired in the beams of the morning' (1836)

'Composed by the Seaside, Near Calais'

Wordsworth, in France, looks across towards England and sees the Evening Star. Both star and country are, he believes, equally glorious and may fittingly be associated with each other.

COMMENTARY: This, and the nine sonnets which follow it, refer to Wordsworth's visit to Calais in 1802 and his return to England. They reflect his fears of renewed French hostility and of English unpreparedness. The Peace of Amiens, signed by Britain and France in 1802, was effective for only fourteen months.

'Calais, August 1802'

The poet, seeing men flocking to pay homage to Napoleon, reminds them that a man who has restricted their liberties is not a fit object of such homage.

COMMENTARY: Napoleon was made Consul in 1799 and Consul for life in 1802. Though he did not become Emperor until 1804 his status in 1802 was already royal in everything except name. The question with which Wordsworth's poem opens is a reference to an incident recorded in the New Testament (see Matthew 11:1–15; Luke 7:24–8). Jesus asks the Jewish crowds whether, when they went out to meet John the Baptist, they expected to see a reed shaken in the wind or a man gorgeously dressed. They expected to see neither of these things, he says, but instead went out to see a prophet. And John, as well as being a prophet, is also the forerunner of the Kingdom of God. By referring to this biblical incident Wordsworth is able to reflect ironically on Napoleon, who, unlike the Baptist, is prophet not of new-found freedom but of an earthly and oppressive kingdom.

'Composed Near Calais on the Road Leading to Ardres'

When Wordsworth and Jones (see p. 6) visited Calais in 1790 France was celebrating Louis XVI's agreement to act within constitutional limits. Wordsworth contrasts the happiness and hope of that time with the disappointment of the present, but without yielding to despair.

'It is a beauteous evening'

The poet believes that his daughter is unconsciously devout, though she is outwardly untouched by the solemn beauty of the evening. (This sonnet is addressed to Wordsworth's daughter, Caroline Vallon, who at the time of his visit was nine years old.)

NOTES AND GLOSSARY:

Abraham's bosom: a reference to the biblical story (see Luke 16:19–31) of Lazarus, who was a poor man, and of the rich man who in this life ignored him. Both men die, and the rich man, in great pain, sees Lazarus resting in comfort upon Abraham's bosom

'On the Extinction of the Venetian Republic'

Wordsworth pays a tribute of respect to the Venetian republic which, once powerful and free, has now fallen under the yoke of Napoleon.

COMMENTARY: In 1797 Austria signed the Treaty of Campo Formio and surrendered to Napoleon. In return Napoleon granted Austria authority over Venice, which he had deprived of its ancient independence earlier in the same year.

NOTES AND GLOSSARY:

a maiden City: notice how Wordsworth carries forward this image: 'seduced', 'violate', 'Mate', 'espouse'

espouse the everlasting Sea: in symbolic recognition of Venice's dependence upon the sea for her prosperity and political standing the Doge (the principal nobleman) used once a year to cast a wedding-ring into the waters of the Adriatic

'To Toussaint L'Ouverture'

The poet tells Toussaint that, although Napoleon has defeated him, the ideals for which he stood will not share in his defeat but will survive for ever.

COMMENTARY: Francois Dominique L'Ouverture (known as Toussaint because he was born on All Saints' Day, 1743) had risen to prominence on his native island of St Domingo after the French had freed the slave population in 1794. When Napoleon sought to reintroduce slavery in 1801 Toussaint resisted. He was captured, was shipped over to France, and was there allowed to die in prison in 1803.

'Composed in the Valley Near Dover'

His return to England, from a Continent which is no longer free, confirms the strength of Wordsworth's love of his own country.

NOTES AND GLOSSARY:

those boys: they were playing cricket, as reference to Dorothy Wordsworth's journal makes clear

by the score: an excellent example of a phrase introduced merely to maintain the rhyme scheme. Presumably Wordsworth means that there were a great many boys playing ('score' means twenty). In this context, however, another meaning of the word (the total of runs made and of wickets taken) cannot be ruled out. Wordsworth recognised the difficulty and later changed lines 4–5 to: 'In white-sleeved shirts are playing; and the roar/ Of the waves breaking on the chalky shore;—/ All, all are English.'

'Near Dover, September 1802'

Wordsworth stands looking towards France. Though the English Channel separates the two countries, and offers welcome protection, England's best defence is a renewed conviction of the value of national liberty.

NOTES AND GLOSSARY:
the barrier flood: the English Channel

'Written in London, September 1802'

Having maintained in the previous sonnet that moral and spiritual integrity is the sole adequate guarantee of freedom, Wordsworth in this sonnet and the next questions whether such integrity is any longer to be found in England.

NOTES AND GLOSSARY:
Plain living: late in life Wordsworth recalled how, upon returning from France in 1802, he had been struck 'with the vanity and parade of our country, especially in great towns and cities'

'London, 1802'

England is morally undeserving of victory and needs to be rescued by a man such as Milton, by a man who is dutiful, independent, proud, and high-principled.

COMMENTARY: Milton's literary influence on Wordsworth has already been discussed in the general note on the sonnets on p. 43. To that account may be added a comment that Wordsworth included in a letter to the poet Walter Savage Landor (1775–1864): 'Many years ago my sister happened to read to me the sonnets of Milton, which I could at that time repeat . . . I was singularly struck with the style of harmony, and the gravity, and republican austerity of those compositions' (20 April 1822).

In this poem Wordsworth has in mind the part that Milton played in bringing to an end the reign of Charles I, executed in 1649. Elsewhere, Wordsworth wrote of 'the moral purity and greatness, and that sanctity of civil and religious duty, with which the tyranny of Charles the first was struggled against'.

'The world is too much with us'

Our self-seeking has robbed us of imagination and is starving us spiritually.

NOTES AND GLOSSARY:
boon: gift
Proteus: one of the sea-gods of ancient Greece
Triton: another sea-god, often depicted blowing on the spiral shell with which he calmed the waters

'Nuns fret not at their convent's narrow room'

Self-imposed constraints may stimulate us more effectively than undisciplined freedom.

NOTES AND GLOSSARY:
Cells: it is possible that the hermits' cells (rooms in which they live and pray) have suggested the image of the bees, whose honeycombs are made up of conjoined hexagonal cells
Furness Fells: a range of hills immediately to the west of the southern quarter of Windermere and six miles south of Hawkshead

'Thought of a Briton on the Subjugation of Switzerland'

The poet addresses Liberty, as though it were a pure young woman, and reminds her that the fall of Switzerland should cause her to cling even more firmly to England.
COMMENTARY: Napoleon's destruction of Swiss liberty was two-fold. In 1798 he invaded the country and in 1802 imposed upon it a government of his own choosing.

NOTES AND GLOSSARY:
Two Voices: Great Britain ('of the sea') and Switzerland ('of the mountains')

'After-thought'

Wordsworth, looking at the Duddon, is reminded that the river will never perish. We are not as fortunate, but must strive to live honourably and to serve future generations as best we can.
COMMENTARY: This is the last of a sequence of thirty-four sonnets

addressed to the River Duddon, the 'partner' and 'guide' of the poem's opening line.

'Inside of King's College Chapel, Cambridge'

We should not resent the spending of money on those products of human skill and art and imagination which serve to show that we are not mere drudges but have an undying future beyond the grave.

COMMENTARY: Wordsworth's *Ecclesiastical Sonnets* form a long history of the English Church, divided into three parts containing thirty-nine, forty-six and forty-seven sonnets respectively. 'Tax not the royal Saint' is the forty-third sonnet in the third part. In November 1820 Wordsworth visited his brother, Christopher, who was Master of Trinity College, Cambridge. This sonnet was written during this visit, or shortly afterwards.

NOTES AND GLOSSARY:

royal Saint: Henry VI (1421–71), son of the famous warrior king, Henry V. The younger Henry proved, in the words of a modern historian, George Holmes, to be 'the exact opposite of his father' and was 'a pious well-intentioned recluse and, later in life, weak-minded. His best memorial is King's College Chapel at Cambridge'

white-robed Scholars only: 'White-robed' because they wear surplices. the long white choir-dress of English clergy and choristers

branching roof: the chapel, built in the perpendicular style of medieval Gothic, is chiefly famous for its elaborate but strictly disciplined roof-vaulting

'Mutability'

The poet reminds us that we should not fix our hearts upon the outward show of things, all of which are destroyed by time and pass into oblivion. This is the thirty-fourth sonnet in the third part of the *Ecclesiastical Sonnets*.

NOTES AND GLOSSARY:

From low to high . . . over-anxious care: the destruction of those things that had once seemed permanent, and the recognition that such destruction is widespread, greet, like solemn but impressive music, the man who is not distracted by crime, greed, or anxiety

touch of Time: Professor Ernest de Selincourt (see Part 5, Sugges-
tions for further reading) has pointed out that the
image with which this poem ends (that of a tower,
crowned with vegetable growth and shattered by
time) and the phrase 'the unimaginable touch of
time' occur in a fragmentary poem written by
Wordsworth in the early 1790s. We thus have a
minor, though elegant, example of Wordsworth's
putting an image into storage for many years

'Scorn not the sonnet'

We should not despise the sonnet, and we shall not do so if we remem-
ber how many great poets have been sonneteers.
COMMENTARY: The references are to William Shakespeare (1564–1616),
Edmund Spenser (1552–99), and John Milton (1608–74); to the Italians,
Dante (1265–1321), Petrarch (1304–74), and Torquato Tasso (1544–
95); and to the Portuguese poet, Luis Vaz de Camoens (1524–80).

NOTES AND GLOSSARY:

an exile's grief: Camoens spent many years travelling in the Orient.
In that respect, but not in any other, he was an exile
a gay myrtle leaf: the myrtle (a small, scented shrub) was sacred to
Venus, goddess of love. Wordsworth means that
Dante's love-sonnets, signalled by the myrtle-leaf,
form only a small part of his total achievement,
which is mostly made up of the sombre magnifi-
cence of the *Divine Comedy*, the greatest of all
Christian allegories
Faeryland: Spenser's longest and most famous work is *The
Faerie Queene*

'On the Departure of Sir Walter Scott'

Wordsworth visited Walter Scott (1771–1832), at Abbotsford, in the
Scottish borders (near the Eildon hills and the River Tweed), in 1831.
Scott, who was seriously ill, was about to travel to Naples (Parthenope)
in the hope that its warmer climate would cure him.
    The departure of Scott from Abbotsford has cast the natural world
into gloom. Wordsworth asks Nature to revive, since Scott is seeking to
recover his health and is aided by friendly winds and the calmness of
the Mediterranean.

'The Trossachs'

The natural world teaches man, as works of art do not, that he is transient.

COMMENTARY: This is another sonnet written, like the previous one, during Wordsworth's visit to Scotland in 1831, and influenced by his sadness over Scott's decline. The Trossachs are the hilly wilderness between Loch Achray and Loch Katrine in Perthshire.

NOTES AND GLOSSARY:

confessional: strictly a place, usually in a church, where a priest hears the confessions of the penitent: here, an appropriate ('apt') place in which to declare that 'Life is but a tale of morning grass/ Withered at eve'

pensive warbler: presumably ('ruddy breast') the robin. An unusually clear example of poetic diction, of a sort that Wordsworth once rejected (in theory, though not always in practice)

This moral: as set out in lines 4 and 5

lay: song

The Excursion

Book VII, 55–290

For a brief account of the relationship between *The Prelude* and *The Excursion*, and between both and *The Recluse*, see the head-note to *The Prelude* (pp. 56–7). Book VII, from which the present extract is taken, consists of histories of his parish told by a clergyman (the Pastor) to the Author and two acquaintances (the Wanderer and the Solitary). When asked to give an account of a group of five graves the Pastor points to a small, deserted cottage, set amongst trees, and tells the story which is here excerpted. An ambitious and hard-living priest, deserted by his influential friends, retreats to a lonely rural parish. There, over the course of many years, he gradually moderates the faults of his temperament.

NOTES AND GLOSSARY:

wain: waggon

the Priest: a clergyman of the Church of England, and thus entitled to marry. Wordsworth based his portrait (though he altered details) on that of a local clergyman, Joseph Sympson, whom he knew well and who lived to be ninety-two

Young was I then: the 'I' is the clergyman who tells the story

with a lady's mien: she had the air and appearance of being a woman of refinement and rank

freak: a piece of unstudied comic action or capriciousness (here designed to keep up the family's spirits as it travels)

Strollers: ballad-versions of the story of Rosamond (mistress of Henry II and thought to have been murdered by Queen Eleanor) and of the Babes in the Wood appear in Thomas Percy's *Reliques of Ancient English Poetry* (1765), the most famous of all eighteenth-century collections of ballads. The strollers presumably 'enact' more substantial, dramatised versions of these. 'Dick Whittington' and 'The Babes in the Wood' survive on the modern English stage as pantomimes (Christmas entertainments designed for children). The 'tabby' is the cat that helps establish Dick Whittington's prosperity

pastoral care: a priest is supposed to look after his congregation as carefully as a shepherd looks after his sheep: hence 'pastoral' care

Champions of the bowl: the bowl is a drinking-bowl, and the priest is as good as any man in drinking from it

Clerk: a clergyman is still known officially as a Clerk (a man who can write) in Holy Orders

patronage: the right to appoint a clergyman to a parish was often owned by a layman, or clergyman, or corporate body, who were known as 'patrons'. Among his drinking friends the priest had been unable to find a patron willing to appoint him to a parish

For a life's stay: for that which would 'stay' (or support) his life

Cure: a priest's responsibility for the spiritual well-being of his people is sometimes known as his 'cure of souls'

His fields: of the people who lived in the remoter valleys in the Lake District, Wordsworth wrote, in his *Guide through the District of the Lakes*, that 'they had . . . their rural chapel, and of course their minister, in clothing or in manner of life, in no respect differing from themselves, except upon the Sabbath-day'

Benefice: a parish, when it is thought of in terms of the money that it brings the priest. This benefice is 'spare' because the priest is not well paid

board: table. The word survives with this meaning in the expression 'bed and board'

To beautify with Nature's fairest growth: 'Both the coverings and sides of the houses have furnished places of rest for the seeds of lichens, mosses, ferns, and flowers' (Wordsworth's *Guide through the District of the Lakes*)

glebe: land belonging to a priest and used to support his family and himself

Miscellaneous poems

'Laodamia'

Laodamia prays to the gods for the return of her dead husband, Protesilaus. She is granted her request, but only for three hours. He tells her, when he returns, that she must moderate her grief and must not cling to him. She disregards his advice and dies when he is reclaimed, but, as a punishment, is not allowed to join the happy spirits in the afterlife.

COMMENTARY: This poem, which is uncharacteristic of Wordsworth both in style and content, cost him, on his own admission, an unusual amount of effort. It is based upon the sixth book of Virgil's *Aeneid* and upon other ancient texts. Protesilaus, King of Phylace in Thessaly, was the first Greek to land at Troy, defying an oracle that predicted that the first who did so would die. His wife, Laodamia, prays to the gods and Protesilaus is returned to her by Hermes, but with the consequences that Wordsworth explains in his poem.

NOTES AND GLOSSARY:

Mercury: the name by which the Romans knew Hermes, the messenger of the gods

Jove: Jupiter, the most important god in Classical mythology

Delphic oracle: the foremost oracle of the Classical Greek world, associated with Apollo, god of prophecy and supporter of the Trojan cause

Hector: a famous Trojan hero, son of Priam, King of Troy

redundant: overflowing, cascading

Parcae: the Fates, three goddesses who supervise the workings of destiny. They are said to be 'conscious' because they know what fate awaits Laodamia

Stygian: the Styx was the river that surrounded the Greek underworld. 'Stygian' means 'gloomy' or 'dark'

Erebus: a part of the Greek underworld, or (as perhaps here) the deity who presides over that part

for the Gods approve . . . of the soul: these lines sum up Wordsworth's message in 'Laodamia'. The thought is one that runs throughout much of his writing

Hercules: Alcestis agreed to take upon herself the fate of her husband and die in his place. Hercules, most famous of all ancient heroes, wrestled with Death and restored Alcestis to her husband

Aeson: the father of Jason, who died while his son was away winning the Golden Fleece. He was restored to life and youth by Medea, a sorceress who was at the time his daughter-in-law

Elysian: Elysium was the dwelling-place after death of those who were blessed

enchained: Professor de Selincourt has shown, by reference to one of Wordsworth's letters, that the word 'enchained' should be followed by a comma, not a full stop. This line and the next are to be taken together: 'The wind that we desired was given to us when ('what time') the fleet lay at Aulis'

I then revolved/ The oracle: 'I turned over in my mind what the oracle had predicted.' 'Silent sea' is perhaps a memory of part of Coleridge's *Ancient Mariner*: 'We were the first that ever burst/ Into that silent sea'

By no weak pity . . . 'mid unfading bowers: this is the reading of 1827. In 1815 Wordsworth had written a very different stanza, in which Laodamia 'in a trance of passion' is 'delivered from the galling yoke of time' and allowed 'to gather flowers/ Of blissful quiet 'mid unfading bowers'. In 1830 Wordsworth explained the change in a letter to his son John: 'As first written the Heroine was dismissed to happiness in Elysium. To what purpose then the mission of Protesilaus—He exhorts her to moderate her passion—the exhortation is fruitless—and no punishment follows. So it stood; at present she is placed among unhappy Ghosts, for disregard of the exhortation. Virgil also places her there'

'Composed upon an Evening of Extraordinary Splendour and Beauty'

An especially beautiful evening revitalises Wordsworth's belief that natural beauty reveals divine glory. That belief, once so strong, has been in abeyance for years, but Wordsworth offers thanks for its temporary return.

NOTES AND GLOSSARY:

effulgence:	radiance (from the Latin word *fulgere*, 'to shine')
scale:	ladder (Latin *scala*); compare 'bright steps' in line 51. Wordsworth claimed that the line 'Wings at my shoulder seemed to play' was inspired by a painting of Jacob's dream. Jacob (see the Bible, Genesis 28:12) dreamt that there was a ladder stretching from heaven to earth, and that angels moved up and down the ladder

---

'Extempore Effusion upon the Death of James Hogg'

The death of a friend and fellow poet brings to Wordsworth's mind the recent deaths of other poets.

COMMENTARY: 'The persons lamented in these verses were all either my friends or acquaintance' (Wordsworth). The poem was written within half an hour (hence 'extempore') of Wordsworth's having read a notice of Hogg's death.

NOTES AND GLOSSARY:

Ettrick Shepherd:	the name by which James Hogg (1770–1835), the Scottish poet, was often known. Wordsworth met him in 1814 when on a Scottish tour
Border-minstrel:	Sir Walter Scott was so called because he compiled a ballad-collection called *Minstrelsy of the Scottish Border* (1802–3). In 1831 Scott showed Wordsworth over the countryside that Hogg had shown him in 1814
Lamb:	Charles Lamb (1775–1834), another of Wordsworth's close literary acquaintances and a celebrated essayist
Crabbe:	George Crabbe (1754–1832), a fine poet, who wrote (often about the lot of the poor in East Anglia) in the manner of the older generation to which he belonged. Wordsworth admired his poetry, but with serious reservations
For Her who:	Felicia Dorothea Hemans (1793–1835), once a celebrated poetess, now remembered only as the author of 'The boy stood on the burning deck' and the originator of the phrase 'The stately homes of England'

The Prelude

The Prelude opens with an account of Wordsworth's escape from the unpleasantness and constraint of town-living into the freer life of the countryside. Rejoicing in his new-found freedom, he dedicates himself to his chosen task, that of writing a major poem. In order not to be unduly ambitious at this early stage, he begins to review his own mind and its abilities, and lists the kinds of poem that he has thought of writing (line 146 onwards). Nevertheless, despite encouraging reports and no lack of subject matter, he finds it at present impossible to write an epic or heroic poem. Instead he carries forward the review of his own mind, and in the remainder of the first book and throughout the second describes his childhood and school days, in order the better to take stock of himself and of his situation, and to show how Nature has shaped his development. (In very early versions of *The Prelude* lines 269–70 of the 1850 text are those with which the poem opens.)

Wordsworth describes his early days at Cockermouth (lines 269–300). He then includes famous accounts of incidents in which he took part when he was a schoolboy: stealing game-birds that others had trapped (lines 306–25); robbing ravens' nests (lines 326–39); taking a boat without permission (lines 357–400); skating (lines 430–63); and playing cards (lines 499–543). He concludes this opening book by admitting that his drooping spirits have been revived by the effort of writing it (lines 636–7).

In the second book of *The Prelude* Wordsworth continues the review of his early years. He remembers the old lady who used to sell cheap goods in Hawkshead (lines 33–56); his sailing trips on Windermere (lines 55–77); his going horse-riding to distant places (lines 94–137); and his visits to an inn where he used to buy strawberries and cream (lines 138–60). At this point Wordsworth ceases to review his past and instead, in the remainder of the second book, attempts to explain his intellectual development by showing how a deeply pondered love of Nature has grown out of the boyish adventures and enthusiasms that he has been describing. (The details of this difficult latter part of Book II are explained step by step in the notes below.)

COMMENTARY: *The Prelude, or Growth of a Poet's Mind; An Autobiographical Poem* was first published, posthumously, in 1850. Its title, suggested by Mrs Wordsworth, recognises the fact that it was never meant to stand by itself but was, instead, the prelude or prolegomenon to a still more massively ambitious poem that was never finished.

That poem, to be known as *The Recluse*, was to be in three parts, the second of which (under the title of *The Excursion*) was published in 1814. Thus the poem, if it had been completed, would have had the following structure: Preliminary Poem (on the making of a poet);

The Recluse, Part I; *The Recluse*, Part II (*The Excursion*); and *The Recluse*, Part III.

The Excursion, though the first (and only) part of *The Recluse* to be written, was, we have seen, intended to figure as the second part of that enormous 'moral and philosophical Poem' whose subject was to be, in the words of the preface to *The Excursion*, whatever Wordsworth found 'most interesting in Nature, Man, and Society'. Such a large venture, large even by Wordsworth's standards, was not to be undertaken lightly, or by a man who was not in possession of himself. There had, inevitably, to be careful preparation, the main part of which was to be the writing of a poem on the 'origin and progress' of Wordsworth's own powers 'as far as he was acquainted with them'. But the task of describing one's moral and emotional progress in detail is such a continuous and continuously fascinating one that it diverted energies from *The Recluse*, and became itself the absorbing enterprise of Wordsworth's maturity. It was 'finished' in 1805 (in a thirteen-book version); was revised during the next thirty years; and appeared, after its author's death, in 1850 (in a fourteen-book version, owing to the division of Book X).

Even in 1805, however, *The Prelude* was not a new poem. Its origins go back at least as far as 1797 when Wordsworth read to Coleridge a poem about one of those hard-pressed women who occur so often in his early verse. In 1798 he lengthened the poem, then known as 'The Ruined Cottage', and eventually transferred much of it to the opening book of *The Excursion*. Certain parts of this early poem, those which concern a character known as The Pedlar, were withheld from *The Excursion* because they had already been put into the early *Prelude*. To these parts Wordsworth added, while he was in Germany, passages of verse in which he recalled his childhood. By 1800 the processes of addition, combination, and composition had advanced so thoroughly that he had written what is really the first version of *The Prelude*.

This early *Prelude*, which has only recently been published, is of considerable interest (and prompts the reflection that Wordsworth is the only Romantic poet who is still producing major poetry). It has two 'parts' and corresponds roughly to the first two books of the 1805 and 1850 versions. It begins, as few readers will be surprised to learn, at line 269 of the 1850 text ('Was it for this . . . ?'), and contains a few passages that were afterwards transferred to later books, but it amply confirms what many had in any case suspected—that the first two books of *The Prelude* form a unity within the larger, and somewhat problematic, unity of the entire poem. There is, finally, some evidence, though no text survives, of yet another version of *The Prelude*, this time in five books and written and dismantled in 1804.

Book I

NOTES AND GLOSSARY:

lines 1–45: these lines (often known as the 'Preamble') were written in 1799 and refer principally to Wordsworth's decision to live in Grasmere. The older belief that they were written in 1795 and refer to his settlement at Racedown is now discredited

visitant: (1850 text) the breeze in 1805 is referred to as a 'welcome messenger' and a 'welcome friend'. By calling it a 'visitant' (a poetical synonym for 'visitor') Wordsworth is able to look forward to other lines in his poem (line 96, for example). Both 'visitant' and 'messenger' suggest the bearer of divine gifts. This suggestion is borne out by 'blessing' (line 1) and 'mission' (line 5) and by many other similar words throughout this opening book

escaped/ From the vast city: the city has been variously identified. By describing it as 'vast' (1850 only) Wordsworth must mean to indicate London, where he had spent several months in 1795 before Calvert's legacy enabled him to travel to Bristol and settle at Racedown. The questions in lines 10–13 refer to Grasmere, but Wordsworth is telescoping the events of 1795 and 1799

The earth is all before me: the first, the most famous, and the most moving of many references to John Milton's *Paradise Lost*. Here Wordsworth is alluding to lines with which the poem ends, and which describe the expulsion of Adam and Eve from paradise: 'The world was all before them, where to choose/ Their place of rest, and providence their guide.' Wordsworth retains Milton's sense of a great adventure, but since he is escaping from a 'vast city', not being expelled from the Garden of Eden, he alters the mood of the lines.

a wandering cloud: Wordsworth combines an image from the natural world, suggesting his new-found freedom, with a reference to the Pillar of Cloud that God sent to guide the Israelites by day to their Promised Land (Exodus 13:20). He thus continues the religious associations of lines 1–5, and of lines 32 ('consecrates'), 45 ('matins' and 'vespers'), 52 ('priestly robe'), and 54 ('holy services')

quickening virtue: life-giving, or enlivening, strength. The passage which follows, down to line 45, is difficult because Wordsworth is using certain words in specialised senses. Thus 'redundant' (line 37) does not mean 'useless' or 'superfluous' but 'overflowing' (itself the original meaning of 'superfluous'). And 'vexing' does not mean 'irritating' or 'thwarting' but means instead 'stirring up into a state of turmoil'. Wordsworth says that when he first began to enjoy his new-found freedom he felt within himself a desire to write which has grown so powerfully that now it is clamouring for release in poetry. He thanks both 'the sweet breath of heaven' and the 'correspondent breeze' since they have not only broken through his winter-deadness but have also brought him promise of a new, creative springtime ('vernal promises')

O Friend!: the poem is addressed throughout to Coleridge

that day: a recent suggestion is that Wordsworth is referring to the period in 1799 after he had shown Coleridge the Lake District and before Dorothy and he had moved into Dove Cottage. 'That day' is probably, therefore, 18 November 1799

Internal echo of the imperfect sound: this line is not often glossed, even though Wordsworth's meaning is not entirely clear. He is probably referring to the fact that we can often (in our heads) reproduce music perfectly, though we cannot reproduce this perfection when called upon to sing. He was cheered both by the poetry which he then composed (the 'measured strains/ That . . . are here/ Recorded') and by his awareness of the still greater poetry within him that had so far eluded composition

a known Vale: the vale of Grasmere, within which Dove Cottage is situated. In a poem known as 'Home at Grasmere', which was to have been included in the first part of *The Recluse*, Wordsworth insists that it was not chance, but prior acquaintance with Grasmere and an already established affection for the place, which brought him there in November 1799. He had, he says, as a schoolboy on a lone trip, seen the valley, had been 'with a sudden influx overpowered' at the sight of its seclusion, and had felt that 'here/ Must be his Home, this Valley be his World' ('Home at Grasmere', lines 44–5)

a higher power/ Than Fancy: imagination. The distinction between Fancy and Imagination, which was especially important in Coleridge's thinking (see his *Biographia Literaria*, Chapter 13), is impossible to indicate in a few words. Both Wordsworth and Coleridge, however, agreed in thinking Imagination vastly superior to Fancy, by virtue of being a truly creative faculty rather than the ability to link together things which only superficially or trivially resembled one another

sere: withered

the curling cloud/ Of city smoke: if 'that day' (line 48) is indeed 18 November 1799 Wordsworth can hardly here be referring to London, which not even a poet could see from Ullswater. Once again it is likely that he is telescoping events of 1795 and 1799. In 1795 he would have left Bristol for Racedown (also in a valley, and also representing escape and security). *The Prelude* is an autobiographical poem, not a road-map, and we need not be surprised by Wordsworth's combining events in this way so as to bring out his meaning more clearly. He has moved from a large city, where he felt restricted and oppressed, into the open and inspiring life of the countryside. That, in reality, this movement was a complicated affair, spread over several years, is a fact which a biographer must remember, but which the author of *The Prelude* is at liberty to forget. 'A backward glance' is another reference to the ending of *Paradise Lost*

Æolian visitations: 'visitations' recalls line 2 of the poem. An æolian harp is one whose strings are played upon by the wind

Sabbath: the Jewish day of rest and spiritual refreshment, upon which no work was to be done

some old/ Romantic tale: Milton had at one time intended to write an epic poem on the life of King Arthur. In lines 170–85 Wordsworth refers to a poem such as Edmund Spenser's *The Fairie Queene*, a long tale of knights, of damsels in distress, and of fantastic adventures, in which aspects of Christian moral thinking are given expression. Edmund Spenser (1552–99) was a major poet of the English Renaissance

Mithridates: Mithridates (131–63BC) was defeated by Pompey, a

Roman general, in 66BC. Wordsworth identifies him with Odin, a legendary chieftain who, in order to escape the power of Rome, took his people northwards into Sweden, where they eventually became known as the Goths. The Gothic armies sacked Rome in AD410

Sertorius: a Roman general, allied to Mithridates, and opposed to Pompey. He was assassinated in 72BC but a very late story records that his followers sought refuge in the Canary Islands, and that their descendants perished bravely during the Spanish invasion of the Canaries in 1493

one Frenchman: 'Dominique de Gourgues, who in 1567 sailed to Florida to avenge the massacre of the French by the Spaniards' (Note in the 1850 edition)

Gustavus: Gustavus I (1496–1560) was King of Sweden, and the man who rid his country of Danish authority. Much of his time was spent in the mining region of Dalecarlia

Wallace: William Wallace (1272?–1305), Scottish patriot who opposed the attempts of the English king, Edward I, to subdue Scotland

Orphean lyre: according to Greek legend Orpheus was such an excellent musician that when he played on the lyre even rocks and trees were compelled to listen to him

interdict: a prohibition. More especially an ecclesiastical ban, used as an extreme punishment, that worked by prohibiting the services of the Church from being performed. Thus Wordsworth carries forward the religious imagery that he so often associates with the act of writing verse

Like a false steward: a reference to the biblical parable (told in Matthew 25:14–30; and Luke 19:11–27) of the servant who received money from his master but who, because he was too timid to invest it, was unable to return more than he had been given. He does, however, return the original loan; either Wordsworth's phrasing is a little misleading, or he wishes to imply that he is even worse than the false steward

the fairest of all rivers: the Derwent, which joins the Cocker at Cockermouth

composed: this word suggests both (musical) 'composition' and physical and moral 'composure'

those towers: the towers of Cockermouth Castle

our terrace walk: this terraced walk at the back of Wordsworth's birthplace still exists

mill-race: a water-channel constructed to divert water from a river in order to operate a mill-wheel

distant Skiddaw's lofty height: Skiddaw (pronounced 'Skidder') is one of the highest of the Lake District mountains and stands ten miles to the east of Cockermouth

belovèd Vale: Esthwaite. Hawkshead, to which Richard and William Wordsworth were removed in 1779, is situated in this valley

springes: nooses or snares in which the feet of game-birds become entangled

fearless visitings: the word recalls 'visitant' (line 2) and 'visitation(s)' (lines 96 and 314). Notice, once again, how a word that has religious associations ('ministry') follows. In 1805 Wordsworth wrote, not 'fearless visitings', but 'gentlest visitation'

One summer evening . . . a trouble to my dreams: a reader of the 1850 text would readily assume that the boat-stealing incident is set on Esthwaite, and might be forgiven for thinking that 'led by her' is a reference either to Dorothy (who was, however, staying in Halifax at this time) or to some other young girl. He would be wrong on both counts. The 1805 text states clearly that the incident took place on Ullswater, a large lake much nearer to Penrith, during Wordsworth's holidays. Furthermore the way in which the verse-paragraph begins in the 1805 text: 'One evening (surely I was led by her)/ I went alone into a Shepherd's Boat', and Wordsworth's description of himself as having 'Forth rambled from the Village Inn alone' make it clear that he had no human companionship, and that it was Nature who led him into the boat in order to forward her 'ministry/ More palpable'

As if with voluntary power instinct: as if of its own accord

The pack loud chiming: the barking or baying of a pack of hunting dogs is sometimes referred to as 'chiming' on a fancied analogy with the ringing of bells. In Shakespeare's *A Midsummer Night's Dream* Theseus' dogs are said to be 'Slow in pursuit, but match'd in mouth like bells' (IV. 1.)

reflex: reflection. In 1805 the word 'image' was used instead

spinning still/ The rapid line of motion: the 'rapid line of motion' is the line cut in the ice by the skate. Wordsworth thinks of it as though it were pulled away from the skate as thread is pulled away from a spinning-wheel

diurnal: see the notes to 'A slumber did my spirit seal', p. 24

Loo or Whist: these are card games. The cards are said to be a 'thick-ribbed army' because their edges have become frayed through frequent use. Wordsworth is here recalling a famous passage in Shakespeare's *Measure for Measure* in which Claudio, faced with the prospect of death, contemplates the horrors of an afterlife where he may have 'to reside/ In thrilling region of thick-ribbed ice' (III. 1.). Notice how Wordsworth recalls the ice, perhaps without realising, in line 539. This Shakespearian image was one that stayed in his mind. In 'The Convict', one of the poems in the 1798 edition of *Lyrical Ballads*, he refers to 'the thick-ribbed walls that o'ershadow the gate'. The lines in *The Ancient Mariner*: 'And thou art long, and lank, and brown/ As is the ribbed sea-sand' were supplied by Wordsworth

Bothnic Main: the Baltic Sea

sedulous: careful

How Nature ... life and joy: the 'severer interventions' that Wordsworth has been describing (in, for example, the boat-stealing episode) are, he believes, a deliberate lesson taught him by nature. He further believes that the changed view of the world which results from this lesson would not have been achieved by him without nature's intervention. Such intervention is thus properly described as being 'extrinsic' (having its origins outside himself). By contrast the 'joys/ Of subtler origin' (the 'calm delight') originate within himself, without the aid of 'ministry/ More palpable', and are evidence that man and the natural world are attuned to each other (by means of their 'first-born affinities')

Organic pleasure: the pleasure which the human organism takes from 'unconscious intercourse' with that greater organism (of nature) of which it is a part. It is a pleasure that is the product not of thought but of an instinctive sensing of man's affinities with the natural world

impending: overhanging (a Latinism)

Of Cumbria's rocky limits: Cumbria is an ancient (and recently revived) name for the counties of Cumberland and Westmorland and the northernmost part of Lancashire

fancies such as these: Wordsworth says that he was then a stranger to the fanciful notion that the sea threw off his evening shade and notified the shepherd's hut of the rising of the moon

No conscious memory: the pleasure that Wordsworth took in the scene was not, he insists, the result of the sort of associations that we all recognise, but was, instead, evidence that the human being, without being wholly aware of it, is attuned to the natural world. Compare Book II, 315–17: 'the soul,/ Remembering how she felt, but what she felt/ Remembering not'

The road lies plain: contrast with Book II, 272–3: 'Yet is a path/ More difficult before me'

Book II

NOTES AND GLOSSARY:

Nor needs: who does not need

One is there: a question ('Is there one?'); Wordsworth's meaning was clearer in the 1805 text: 'And is there one, the wisest and the best/ Of all mankind, who does not sometimes wish/ For things which cannot be . . . ?'

corporeal frame: body

Which . . . mind: which, nevertheless, I remember so vividly

our small market village: Hawkshead. The assembly room was built in 1790

huckster's wares: cheap goods, such as pedlars sell

when the winning forms . . . boyish sport: Wordsworth means that (with the exception of those moments of instinctive admiration of nature mentioned at the end of Book I) the boy is chiefly interested in the natural world (of water, rocks, and the weather) as the setting for his childish play ('boyish sport'), but that the pleasure which such activity brings him is associated with ('collaterally attached' to) the natural world, which itself becomes an object of pleasure. Compare Book I, 599–612, and the notes on 'Tintern Abbey', pp. 19–21.

umbrageous: shady

Our Lady: St Mary the Virgin, to whom many churches and chapels were dedicated in medieval England

Sabine fare!: wholesome and simple food, such as the Roman poet Horace enjoyed on his Sabine farm and praised in his satires

stipend: usually money paid to a parish clergyman: here used humorously to refer to the pocket-money granted to the Wordsworth brothers. The fourth division of the year was taken up by the school holidays, in June and July and over the Christmas season

Druids: the priests of Celtic Britain. Several ruins, popularly thought to be druidical, exist in the Lake District

that large abbey: Furness Abbey, twenty miles from Hawkshead

chauntry: Wordsworth seems here to be using the word loosely, and to refer to that part of the church in which the choir sings

the cross-legged knight: effigies of knights with their legs crossed are not uncommon. Traditionally, though incorrectly, they are thought to represent crusaders

Winander: Windermere, largest of the lakes in this area, and only a few miles from Hawkshead

A tavern stood: the White Lion (later called The Royal) at Bowness

the Hall: a reference to the circular house (thought by some visitors to resemble a tea-canister) built on Belle Isle, largest of the islands in Windermere, in the 1770s. Dorothy Wordsworth was one of many people who disliked it: 'And that great house! Mercy upon us! if it *could* be concealed, it *would* be well for all who are not pained to see the pleasantest of earthly spots deformed by man. But it *cannot* be covered. Even the tallest of our old oak trees would not reach to the top of it' (*Journal*, 8 June 1802)

Minstrel of the Troop: Robert Hodgson Greenwood who, in 1786, boarded with Ann Tyson

In many a thoughtless hour: characteristic of Wordsworth is the ambiguous placing of this phrase, which suggests, until one is compelled to cancel the suggestion, that it is the mountain which is thoughtless, and thus helps Wordsworth evoke, without making him assert, the aliveness of the natural world

For its own pleasure: 'With its own pleasure' in 1805. Changed presumably to avoid the appearance of 'with' twice in the same line

To patriotic and domestic love/ Analogous: 'just as I love *my* country and *my* home so I love not the moon but *my* moon, and think of her "as if she knew/ No other region"'

Those incidental charms . . . her own sake: Wordsworth is here, once again, speaking of the 'collateral attachment' (see line 51 and also my notes on 'Tintern Abbey'). His love of Nature, secondary until this time and having an effect on him only in association with 'every scheme of holiday delight', gradually as he grows older increases in power and ceases to need such association

I hasten on to tell: in fact Wordsworth allows himself a lengthy digression. He does not resume the matter here anticipated until line 272

succedaneum: anything that one falls back on for want of something better; a substitute

Blest the infant Babe . . . violence or harm: in broadest outline, Wordsworth is saying that we come to terms with the world (make sense of it) because we do not approach it as though it were something distinct from ourselves, existing in unmeaning confusion all around us, but instead build up our knowledge of it gradually in terms of those things which we already know. And what we know as children is that we have someone who loves us and whom we may trust. Such love and trust provide the stable basis upon which we may build up our understanding of the world. In short, knowing one relationship (that which we have, as infants, with our mothers), we increase in knowledge of those other relationships that, in total, constitute the world. (In 1805 Wordsworth's argument at this point was a little more explicit, and also slightly different)

creator and receiver both: though the child does not merely create the world (there is a world 'out there', which is the 'world of all of us') its experience of the world is its own: it is not a mere recording drudge, but interprets experience in the act of recording it. Such interpretation is imaginative, and as we grow older we, unless we are poets, take it less and less seriously. By way of clarification we might remind ourselves that certain child-psychologists, in our own century, have claimed that children ascribe animal consciousness to inanimate things: children's books traditionally provide faces for railway engines and motor-cars. And even adults speak, almost without thinking, of the world of external nature in terms of bodily analogies: the foot of a mountain, brow of a hill, mouth of a river, head of a stream, and the teeth, or eye, of a storm. This seeing objects around us as equals to us in consciousness is a stage of development through which all men pass as children and to which, occasionally and in fancy, many men return. 'Am I fanciful', Wordsworth asked Coleridge, with reference to his garden at Dove Cottage, 'when I would extend the obligation of gratitude to insensate things?' (December 1799)

The chamois' sinews: the chamois is a sure-footed antelope, admirably adapted to life in the hilly country which it inhabits

The props of my affections: often glossed as a reference to the death of Wordsworth's parents: what then are we to make of the trouble that 'came into my mind/ From unknown causes'? It may alternatively be supposed that these props are the 'incidental charms' of line 198. These, which had brought into his mind the landscape with which they were associated, had 'day by day grown weaker'. Eventually they are removed, and yet the landscape, which had previously been remembered only because of its association with them, remains, and replaces them in Wordsworth's affections

but that the soul . . . remembering not: perhaps a reference to the pre-existent soul (see 'Ode: Intimations'); more probably a reference to the soul of the child. Whichever is meant, what the soul obscurely recollects is that it was once intimately attuned to the natural world —a recollection which prompts it to recover that condition (of 'sublimity')

that universal power . . . virtue not its own: a very difficult passage, not least because of our not knowing how to attach 'a virtue not its own' to the statement which it concludes. ('Virtue' means 'power' or 'strength'.) 'Its' presumably refers to the 'universal power', and Wordsworth is saying that the mind's perfectly natural delight in the world (a genuine delight, though obscure in its origins) is increased for him by the fact that, because he has not 'abated or suppressed' his childish (and imaginative) understanding of things, his soul can still remember the child's feeling of oneness with the natural world

a Friend: 'The late Rev. John Fleming, of Rayrigg, Windermere' (1850). Fleming, who died in 1835, was another of Wordsworth's Hawkshead schoolmates

prospect: as well as being anything that one sees, or something that one looks forward to, 'prospect' was an eighteenth-century technical term for a stretch of countryside that a landscape painter might wish to depict. The search for suitable prospects became very fashionable. By using the term Wordsworth is able to suggest, wittily, that it is interior landscapes in which he is interested

by the regular . . . unsubdued: see the note on 'Ode: Intimations', lines 144–63 on p. 41

plastic: formative

auxiliar light: this could be equated with the 'virtue not its own' of line 329

a toil: the 'observation of affinities' of line 384

To unorganic natures . . . enjoyments: that Wordsworth was still engaging in such transference at the age of twenty-nine is shown in the letter to which I refer in my note on line 258. 'Unorganic' here means: non-human ('all that moves'), inanimate ('all that seemeth still'), and abstract (that 'liveth to the heart'). Wordsworth means that he thinks of animals, rocks, stones, trees, and even obscure feelings as being fully as much alive as he is himself

Wonder not . . . eye of love: in 1805 Wordsworth had written: 'Wonder not/ If such my transports were; for in all things/ I saw one life, and felt that it was joy.' Wordsworth rewrote the passage in order to emphasise his religious orthodoxy. The 'Uncreated' is God

fleshly ear: just as the eye cannot see the best visions (compare line 352 and note) so the ear cannot hear the best harmonies

my Friend!: Coleridge, once more

To serve . . . to mankind: the unity of the first two books is emphasised by a return to the religious imagery ('serve', 'temple', 'ministers', 'devotion') employed at the beginning of Book I. Notice especially the word 'blessing' which occurs in the opening line of the first book and the closing line of the second

Part 3

Commentary

What is a 'Lyrical ballad'?

First, let us remind ourselves of how *Lyrical Ballads* originated. In 1797 Wordsworth and his sister were living at Alfoxden in Somerset, and in November of that year they joined Coleridge in a walking tour through Devon. In order to recoup their expenses the two men decided to join together in writing a poem ('The Rime of the Ancient Mariner'). The collaboration did not work out, and the poem which resulted was almost entirely Coleridge's, but they nevertheless decided that a different form of collaboration might work better. *Lyrical Ballads*, published anonymously in 1798, was a consequence of that decision. That the collaboration was to be close, and not unlike that which had failed when applied to the 'Ancient Mariner', is indicated by a letter which Coleridge sent to Joseph Cottle, their friend and prospective publisher: 'We deem,' Coleridge wrote, 'that the volumes offered to you are to a certain degree *one work* . . . and that our different poems are as stanzas, good relatively rather than absolutely' (May/June 1798; despite 'volumes' it is the one-volume *Lyrical Ballads* to which reference is being made).

We do not know whether it was Wordsworth or Coleridge or both together who decided what their joint volume of poetry was to be called (strictly: *Lyrical Ballads, With a Few Other Poems*). Nevertheless we must try to find out why the title was chosen, and what a 'lyrical ballad' is. From the very earliest days, indeed, an oddity in the title was noticed. 'The title of the *Poems* is, in some degree, objectionable,' wrote John Wilson, who was one of Wordsworth's most enthusiastic admirers, 'for what *Ballads* are not *lyrical*?' (24 May 1802). And Wilson's question, as befits that of a future professor in a Scottish university, reveals great good sense. Despite Wordsworth's claim that he had called in 'the assistance of lyrical and rapid metre' in writing his ballads, it is hard to imagine anyone wanting to sing 'The Thorn' or 'Ruth' or 'The Complaint of a Forsaken Indian Woman', or passionately reciting them to the accompaniment of a harp. This definition of 'lyric' is Wordsworth's own. In his Preface (1815) he lists six types of poetic writing, the third of which is the 'Lyrical'—'containing the Hymn, the Ode, the Elegy, the Song, and the Ballad; in all which, for the production of their *full* effect, an accompaniment of music is indispensable'. 'Some of these pieces,' he said of *Poems, including Lyrical Ballads*

(1815), 'are essentially lyrical; and therefore cannot have their due force without a supposed musical accompaniment; but in much the greatest part . . . I require nothing more than an animated or impassioned recitation, adapted to the subject'. The problem, therefore, remains: if all ballads are lyrical, then the word 'lyrical' is redundant as a qualifier. Was Wordsworth (or whoever chose the title) merely being tautologous? If we define the 'lyric' a little more liberally than Wordsworth did in 1815 we can see that the title *Lyrical Ballads* is not so obviously flawed. A ballad, if we take the ballads of the Scottish borders as our standard, is a narrative poem, arranged in stanzas, and with a regular and usually simple rhyme-scheme. And a narrative poem is, obviously, one in which incident follows upon incident: in the Border Ballads frequently one violent incident following hard upon the heels of another. But it soon becomes clear from even a casual reading that, though they often tell a story, Wordsworth's lyrical ballads do not exist merely in order to do so. They are poems 'descriptive of human nature', and in such poems, as Wordsworth pointed out to Coleridge in a letter in 1798, 'character is absolutely necessary'. By contrast, 'incidents', he remarks in the same letter, 'are among the lowest allurements of poetry'.

Though a 'lyric' is strictly a poem written to be accompanied on a lyre, that rigid definition rapidly fell away, until in Wordsworth's day, as in ours, a 'lyric' could be simply a poem in which the poet expresses (or at least claims to express) his own thoughts or sentiments or feelings. If we put 'lyric' and 'ballad' together we might, not altogether unreasonably, expect to achieve a poem, written in a narrative mode, in which the unfolding of the story is subordinate in interest and dignity to the expression of the poet's thoughts and feelings, or (as seems to me to be true of Wordsworth's lyrical ballads) a narrative poem in which the unfolding of the story is subordinate in interest and importance to the depiction of the thoughts and feelings of the characters who operate within the poem.

Thus we may summarise the Preface to *Lyrical Ballads* in the following terms. From poems generally esteemed in his own day (poems characterised by an excess of poetic diction) Wordsworth's will be distinguished by superior plainness of style. betokening greater sinerity of purpose and accuracy of observation. From superficially similar narrative or ballad-like poems (of which there were many) his may be distinguished by their 'worthy' purpose, which is to 'illustrate the manner in which one's feelings and ideas are associated in a state of excitement', and by the fact that in them 'the feeling . . . gives importance to the action and situation and not the action and situation to the feeling'. They are called 'Lyrical Ballads' in order to distinguish them from poems whose object is primarily narrative, and to emphasise their concern with the depiction of human feelings. 'The Thorn', for example, is properly a 'Lyrical Ballad' because it is a contribution to the 'history or science of feelings'—more especially it exhibits 'some of the general laws by which superstition acts upon the mind'. It is, therefore, a poem with a purpose (it sets out to instruct as well as to delight) and is, Wordsworth claims, different from those 'idle and extravagant stories in verse' which he holds in such contempt.

A 'Lyrical Ballad', in Wordsworth's estimation, is something other than a mere story in verse in which the human figures are depicted only in such detail as will serve to fill out the story. Instead, the story itself is of little interest, and is chosen because it provides the means by which the 'characters' of the human figures, in their various shades of distress and resignation, can be illustrated and our understanding of them, and of those like them, increased. (Most of the quotations used in this section have been taken from the Preface to *Lyrical Ballads*. You should re-read this preface (Evans, pp. 179–205) in order to restore the quotations to their proper contexts.)

Is Wordsworth a nature poet?

Nature being what it is, all poets are nature poets: so we have to decide not whether Wordsworth is one but rather what sort of one he is.

He is certainly not a camera-on-legs or a singing paintbrush. Wordsworth would 'never have had any great effect on me', John Stuart Mill confessed, 'if he had merely placed before me beautiful pictures of natural scenery. Scott does this still better than Wordsworth, and a very second-rate landscape does it more effectually than any poet'. Why then did Mill read Wordsworth with such pleasure and profit? The answer is prompt: because his verse expresses 'not mere outward beauty, but states of feeling, and of thought coloured by feeling, under the excitement of beauty'.

As far as the negative part of his statement goes Mill is obviously right: we do not read Wordsworth in order to be presented with vivid word-pictures of rocks, stones, trees, birds, flowers, lakes, sunsets, storms, or ripening fields. Indeed, considering his reputation as the most ostentatiously capitalised of all our Nature Poets, it is a genuine surprise to discover how little of his verse is merely descriptive: among near-contemporaries William Cowper (1731–1800) and John Clare (1793–1864) yield a much higher return. Furthermore Mill is not saying anything that Wordsworth was not prepared to say of (and for) himself. Scott, Wordsworth claimed, 'confounds *imagery* with *imagination*':

> Sensible objects really existing, and felt to exist, are *imagery*; and they may form the materials of a descriptive poem, where objects

are delineated as they are. Imagination is a subjective term: it deals with objects not as they are, but as they appear to the mind of the poet.*

Positively, too, Mill is right and in agreement with Wordsworth, whose poetry is concerned to communicate 'states of feeling' ('It is the hour of feeling') and to evoke objects in the natural world 'as they appear to the mind of the poet'. Always the mind of the poet is pre-eminent, or at least a partner: never passive, nor prostrate, nor overborn 'as if the mind/ Itself were nothing, a mean pensioner/ On outward forms' (*Prelude*, 1805, VI, lines 666–8). The 'prospect' that Wordsworth seeks to depict is an interior landscape, a 'prospect in the mind' (*Prelude*, II, line 352: see note, p. 68).

'Poetry is the image of man and nature', Wordsworth claims in the Preface to *Lyrical Ballads*: the poet 'considers man and nature as essentially adapted to each other'. This dual emphasis (on man and on nature, and on both as adapted to, and acting upon, each other) is maintained throughout Wordsworth's best verse: where it is not maintained we have a ready index of the verse's decline. 'Ode: Intimations' posits a time when, between the pre-existent Soul and Nature, there existed an intimacy of union that a man's growth to earthly maturity merely serves to lessen (though Wordsworth insists that a sober estimate of the matter will not dwell only upon this loss: 'We will grieve not, rather find/ Strength in what remains behind'). The first two books of *The Prelude*, without benefit of the pre-existence myth, also dwell upon Man and Nature, and show in great and vivid detail how Nature educated Wordsworth, by means of reprimand and incentive and of quiet, barely noticed, but unremitting pressure. And also *The Prelude* shows how the human mind reaches out and grasps the natural world. Nature's ministry, he tells us, impressed upon caves, trees, woods, and hills, and upon all other forms 'the characters/ Of danger and desire' (Book I, lines 468–72). Sometimes this humanised landscape is thought of as being something which the human mind itself initiates:

Coercing all things into sympathy
To unorganic natures were transferred
My own enjoyments

(Book II, lines 390–2)

And again, in Book III, 1805, lines 124–7:

To every natural form, rock, fruit or flower,
Even the loose stones that cover the highway,

*Christopher Wordsworth, *Memoirs of William Wordsworth*, 2 vols, London, 1851, II, 477.

> I gave a moral life: I saw them feel,
> Or linked them to some feeling.

Wordsworth is not simply the poet of the world that man observes, but of man the observer, of the act of observation itself, of the relationship between Man and Nature, and of the modifications to our understanding of both that observation of each in relation to the other makes necessary.

For such observation the bodily senses are not enough; we need an inward and not a fleshly ear, an inward and not a fleshly eye, and the heart, that most naturally inward of all our organs, must reach levels of versatility to which even the most demanding of bodily athletes never subject it. Some of Wordsworth's most feeling lines are those in which he speaks to us of the heart and its blood. Leonard and James, in 'The Brothers', 'had much love to spare,/ And it all went into each other's hearts'. We know from Dorothy Wordsworth's journals that the heart was very much in Wordsworth's thoughts when he began 'Michael': the sheepfold, she tells us, was 'built nearly in the form of a heart unequally divided'. Or consider two closely linked examples from 'The Brothers' that together compose what is perhaps the most powerful single passage of verse that Wordsworth wrote:

> For five long generations had the heart
> Of Walter's forefathers o'erflowed the bounds
> Of their inheritance

and this:

> Each struggled, and each yielded as before
> A little—yet a little—and old Walter,
> They left to him the family heart.

(Part of the strength of this last line must come to us from the word 'hearth' that is so very nearly, but not quite, there.) Thus we have a heart that overflows (and in *The Prelude* Wordsworth refers to the heart as a 'dimpling cistern': Book V, 1805, line 345), and another that is passed down from father to son like the family bible. Here is one that is an inward eye, watching and receiving:

> Enough of science and of art;
> Close up these barren leaves;
> Come forth, and bring with you a heart
> That watches and receives.

Wordsworth is a nature poet, but not one who ever lets us forget that man is an occupant of the natural world, and that the poet is a man whose duty is to speak to other men. *Lyrical Ballads* are nature poems written in order to illustrate in simple verse 'the primary laws of our nature'. *The Prelude* is a nature poem which depicts the 'Growth of a Poet's Mind'. Every poem that Wordsworth wrote is principally an appeal to that human nature that is shared by both the poet and his readers.

Part 4

Hints for study

Preparing for an examination

The following notes are designed especially for younger students who are preparing for their first public examination, and also for more senior students who suffer from examination nerves and who lose confidence in themselves whenever they are asked to write for a set number of hours in examination conditions. However all students, even the lucky few who are confident of their own abilities, are advised to look carefully at the specimen questions at the end of these hints.

The first point to be made about examinations, of whatever sort, is that they are best regarded as the natural conclusion to a course of study. A question on Wordsworth is designed to test the quality of your understanding of his work, developed over a long period of time. It is not designed to test how many of his poems you have managed to commit to memory in the preceding few days.

From this simple initial point a few equally simple conclusions may be drawn. Preparation for an exam is not a special sort of activity that you undertake once you have stopped reading Wordsworth and thinking about him, and it is not moreover an activity that you should confine to the last few weeks (or, worse still, the last few days) of your academic term or year. In English studies, especially, the mere swot is at a disadvantage. There are no formulas to be learned, or lists of irregular verbs to be mastered, and the committing to memory of a few poems, though often a useful exercise, is not sufficient to guarantee success in an examination.

This last point needs to be looked at more carefully since many students think that an examination is designed to test their knowledge of an author, and think, in addition, that 'knowing an author' equals 'being able to recite the words that he has written'. But an examination is properly designed to test the *quality* of your understanding of an author's work, and merely reciting his words, however accurately, will not satisfy the requirements of such a test. What matters is whether the words which you quote support and illustrate and advance your argument. If they do not they are irrelevant and ought not to be included. You will not see the question until the examination begins, and you cannot answer a question until you have been asked it. It is in the examination itself, therefore, that you will need to recollect those parts

of Wordsworth's poems that are relevant to your answer: the danger
with learning poems, or lists of quotations, by heart a few days before
the examination is that you will include them in your answer merely
because you know them, without regard to their relevance.

Many students are worried when they are told that they will have to
think during an examination: but clearly an examination which did not
require you to think would not be worth sitting, and any qualifications
to which it might lead would not be worth having. What lies behind this
common worry, of course, is the fear that the mind will go blank as
soon as the examination room is entered; but for most students this is
not a real danger provided that preparation has been thorough. This
takes time, and cannot be hurried, but since good preparation is
indistinguishable from a serious and interested reading of your text it
is pleasurable and its own reward, quite apart from the benefits which
it confers in the examination room.

Your success in answering a question on Wordsworth will depend
upon the quality of your reading of his poems. Improving the quality of
your reading is the best way of preparing for an examination. But what
is good reading? And how is reading to be improved?

First of all, good reading is informed. You need to know (and this
book is designed to tell you) when Wordsworth lived, where he lived,
something of what happened during his lifetime, what he thought about
poetry, and what other people thought about it too. Secondly, good
reading is questioning. The good reader asks himself questions like the
following: What do these lines mean? (It's surprising how many people
seem *never* to ask this question.) Is the meaning clearly expressed? Or is
it difficult to puzzle out? Why is it difficult to puzzle out? Do I believe
that what Wordsworth is saying here is true? Have I had experiences
which confirm the truth of what he is saying? Can I think of another
poet who says these same things? Or who says them better? Or who
contradicts them? Why does Wordsworth say these things in verse?
Would a prose account of them be more, or less, effective? Why would
it be more, or less, effective? Does such a prose account exist?

Being willing to ask these questions matters more than being able
to answer them. You should not forget that having a supply of ques-
tions that you cannot yet answer is an excellent reason for re-reading a
poet's works.

Good reading is questioning. Exams, I have claimed, ask questions.
In short they do nothing which you should not have been doing for
yourself for months before entering the examination room. And if you
have been asking yourself questions, and trying to answer them, as a
normal part of your study of Wordsworth, you will certainly find, as you
sit your examination, that appropriate quotations from his poems will
spring into your mind as your answer progresses. Such quotations (they

are often very brief) are what your examiner wants to see: they show that you know your text, and also that you know how to apply your knowledge.

Preparing an essay

The basis of a good examination answer is a sound essay-writing technique, for such an answer, though it will probably be shorter, less detailed, and a little simpler in structure than a classroom essay, will in essentials resemble it closely. We need to discover what makes an essay good: once again common sense is our best guide.

Your essay will be produced in response to a question or request. Here are two examples:

(1) How does Wordsworth, in the 'Lucy Poems', seek to make us share his sense of human loss?
(2) Discuss Wordsworth's depiction of human loneliness and suffering.

The question or request will itself tell you, directly or indirectly, which of Wordsworth's poems should command your attention. In the first, admittedly very simple, example, though you may mention other poems in passing (to establish contrasts and comparisons), the bulk of your answer should be given over to the poems mentioned in the question. The second example is slightly more difficult, since it does not name a specific group of poems, but obviously 'The Female Vagrant', 'The Complaint of a Forsaken Indian Woman' and 'Ruth' should feature more prominently in your answer than 'Tintern Abbey' or the 'Ode to Duty'.

Having decided, by carefully reading the question, which poems are going to provide the raw material of your answer, you need next to decide how you are going to make use of them. The first question, you will notice, does not invite you to write down everything that you know about the Lucy Poems, nor are you simply being asked to state why you like or dislike them. You will need to re-read the poems (if you are writing an ordinary essay) or review them in your mind (if you are in an examination room, without books), paying particularly close attention to lines in which Wordsworth seems to anticipate his loss:

> 'O mercy!' to myself I cried,
>   If Lucy should be dead!

and to lines in which that loss is explicitly stated:

> But she is in her grave, and oh!
>   The difference to me.

or:

> She died, and left to me
> This heath; this calm and quiet scene

and also to lines in which that loss is obliquely registered:

> No motion has she now, no force;
>   She neither hears nor sees

('obliquely registered' because these lines, from 'A slumber did my spirit seal', are only seen to be about Lucy, who is not mentioned in this poem, when the other Lucy Poems are brought to bear upon it. When we consider it by itself, what is to prevent our believing this to be a poem about Wordsworth's spirit, which he addresses as though it were female?)

You will have noticed that the lines cited occur late in their poems, and twice are the lines with which the poems end. Since nothing can end until it has begun, we might now ask ourselves how Wordsworth begins his poems, and how he moves from their beginning to their end. Indeed one way of answering this first question would be by discussing how Wordsworth builds up his poems so as to achieve these endings. How, for example, does he create a sense of foreboding in 'Strange fits of Passion'? An adequate answer would have at least three parts: he does so by means of his poem's first word ('Strange'); by means of the past tense in 'When she I loved *was* strong and gay', which suggests that she may be such no longer; and by means of fixing his own eye, and his reader's attention, hypnotically upon the moon, which features in all except the first and last stanzas, and which is traditionally a symbol not only of love but also of instability. Consider, also, in 'She dwelt among th'untrodden ways', the contrast between the fragile imagery ('a violet by a mossy stone', 'Fair as a star') and the simple statement of her death ('she is in her grave') and of the poet's loss ('and oh!/ The difference to me'). Violets, we remember, lose their scent; stars fall; moss, as in Wordsworth's poem 'The Thorn', is associated with death; and 'stone', in this context, brings to mind graves and their headstones.

If you think about the Lucy Poems along these lines you will soon come up with a handful of points that you wish to make, together with short quotations which will help you to illustrate them. Though a handful of points may not seem very many, it is enough since you are trying to write a good essay, not a long one.

Once you have decided what your essay should contain you must decide what shape it should have. You might, if you were answering this first question, wish to begin with a very brief introduction in which you say that the Lucy Poems have been given this name by readers of Wordsworth's poetry because they are poems in which the poet mourns the death of a young girl whom he calls Lucy. The poet, by the use of the natural imagery that he applies to her, suggests that she is a child of Nature, whom Nature reclaims. The poet is left to mourn his loss, which he does not minimise, and writes his poems in order to revive his memory of her by recollecting the places where she lived and the features of the natural world with which she invited comparison.

Each of the points in this simple introduction (of about one hundred words) can be illustrated from the poems. The central, longest part of your essay should consist of repeating these points, one by one, in order to develop and illustrate them. The quotations from the poems need be only very brief, and may be included within parentheses after the points which they illustrate. You may, however, in order to make your essay more varied, wish to concentrate on one poem in particular and, provided the poem is short (no more than eight or, at most, twelve lines long), it is permissible to write it out in full as a part of your answer. But do not forget that you must discuss the poem. You will receive no marks merely for having remembered it.

You are now ready to finish your essay. A simple ending is always best. Often a single sentence is all that is needed, and, if you have answered the question fairly, you may with a clear conscience allude to its wording in your concluding sentence ('In these ways Wordsworth seeks to make us share his sense of human loss'). But make sure that you have answered the question fairly. Nothing is more annoying to a reader of your essay than a conclusion in which you claim to have done what you have not done.

Some trial questions

Essay-writing is not a natural activity (neither is cooking meat, nor playing cricket, nor switching on an electric light) and it does require you to discipline yourself. We all, however, have the ability to write good, simple essays. Test yourself by working through the second example given earlier. Then work through some of these questions:

(1) Byron thought that Wordsworth's 'performances since *Lyrical Ballads* are miserably inadequate to the ability which lurks within him'. Compare and contrast *Lyrical Ballads* and *Poems* (1807) so as to bring out the truth or falsehood of Byron's comment.

(2) Do you agree that Wordsworth is 'at his best when describing his own childhood'?

(3) Is Wordsworth a simple poet?

(4) Why did Wordsworth revise his poems so often? Did he improve them? (You may, if you wish, say that sometimes he improved them and that sometimes he did not; but you must give examples. The notes in Part 2 ought to help you.)

(5) Wordsworth praised the dignified simplicity and majesty of Milton's sonnets. Do his own sonnets deserve similar praise?

(6) Which of Wordsworth's later poems (those written after 1810) do you think most successful? Why?

(7) Discuss Wordsworth's skills as a *narrative* poet.

(8) What difficulties do you think that the modern reader will encounter when he begins to read Wordsworth's poetry? How are these difficulties best overcome?

(9) What did Wordsworth mean when he said that we should let Nature be our teacher?

(10) 'Poetry is the image of Man and Nature' (Wordsworth). Discuss Wordsworth's poetry in the light of this statement.

Specimen answers

(1) Is Wordsworth a 'pastoral poet'?

Most of the poetry which literary critics term 'pastoral' was either written in classical antiquity or is a modern imitation of ancient poetry. The shepherds and shepherdesses of the pastoral tradition devote their time to singing and dancing and to love-play, not to the serious business of making sure that their flocks are well fed, well watered, and secure.

Judged by the standards of such poetry Wordsworth is not a pastoral poet, and yet he labelled several of his poems as 'pastorals'. Chief among these is 'Michael', which is said to be a pastoral because it is a story about a shepherd (Latin *pastor*, shepherd). Wordsworth, however, has in his mind not the insubstantial lovers of classical antiquity (called Corin, or Damon, or Tityrus) but the shepherds of the biblical Old Testament narratives: Michael is a Hebrew name, not one drawn from the Greek or Roman poets.

Thus it is only by means of a kind of pun, or serious joke, that Wordsworth can be said to be a pastoral poet. He takes a term that ordinarily is applied to extremely mannered and artificial poems and instead applies it to a poem about real-life shepherds of the England of his time. These men, unlike their classical counterparts, are not perpetually young, have financial troubles, and problems with their children. They move through a recognisably English landscape, and through typically English weather. Michael:

> had been alone
> Amid the heart of many thousand mists,
> That came to him, and left him on the heights.

Above all, to these men, sheep and the land which they graze are the means by which money is earned and a family supported. Though there is much real joy ('The pleasure which there is in life itself') there is little time for dancing, or for weaving flowers into young girls' hair, or for drinking sparkling wine:

> two wheels she had
> Of antique form; this large, for spinning wool,
> That small for flax; and if one wheel had rest,
> It was because the other was at work.

Whether we decide that Wordsworth is not a pastoral poet, or that he is a pastoral poet of an unusual kind, is no great matter. What does matter is that we recognise the skill with which he depicts the dignified and often sorrowful lives of his shepherds. His not following pastoral precedent in no way reduces the dignity of his shepherds, and sometimes their dignity and their sorrow exist together in a single image that is beyond the reach of more conventional pastoral. Though Michael does not finish his sheepfold, and on many days can do no work at all, he never entirely gives up the task of building it:

> He at the building of this Sheep-fold wrought,
> And left the work unfinished when he died.

---

(2) How well does Wordsworth succeed in enlisting our human sympathies?

Wordsworth wrote, in his Preface to *Lyrical Ballads*, that the 'feeling' developed in his poems gives 'importance to the action and situation, and not the action and situation to the feeling'. Thus 'The Complaint of a Forsaken Indian Woman', a poem which he had especially in mind, was written not for the sake of its story (which is not, as we commonly understand the term, an 'exciting' one) but in order to excite our sympathies with the Indian Woman as she faces the pains of separation and of imminent death.

In particular Wordsworth wants to enlist our sympathies for the Indian Woman as she alternates between hope and hopelessness. Such rapid alternation, characteristic of the human mind in extremity of distress, is well represented in stanza 6. The first part of the stanza:

> I'll follow you across the snow,
> You travel heavily and slow:
> In spite of all my weary pain,
> I'll look upon your tents again

is followed swiftly by the second, and contrasting, part:

> My fire is dead, and snowy white
> The water which beside it stood;

> The wolf has come to me to-night,
> And he has stolen away my food.

The opening lines of the fourth stanza are very touching also, and are deliberately placed there in order to enlist our sympathies:

> My child! they gave thee to another,
> A woman who was not thy mother.

The second line, which contains only a small amount of new information and which makes room for something that is obvious ('who was not thy mother'), allows us to watch the Indian Woman drawing out for herself the painful implications of the first line: not only is she dying, not only is her child taken away from her, but she is also being replaced. Her loss of her child is also the child's loss of its mother. The mother, in very proper maternal fashion, cannot distinguish the two losses from each other with any clarity, a point which Wordsworth makes again at the end of the poem when the 'Forsaken Indian Woman' laments her 'poor forsaken child'.

Wordsworth tries to enlist our human sympathies because he believes, as most wise men have, that we grow emotionally through the exercise of fellow-feeling. A capacity for such feeling is in all of us: the Poet, Wordsworth tells us in his Preface, principally directs his attention to 'knowledge which all men carry about with them' and to sympathies in which, by our life in the everyday working world, 'we are fitted to take delight'. Provided that we read his verse carefully and allow our own experience to illuminate it, we shall find our powers of sympathy enlisted (as in 'The Complaint of a Forsaken Indian Woman') and then enlivened and, eventually, enlarged.

---

(3) Discuss Wordsworth's depiction in *The Prelude* of one of his child-hood adventures, and show how it plays a part in the overall scheme of the poem.

The Prelude is subtitled 'Growth of a Poet's Mind', and is Words-worth's attempt at showing how a child's imagination is awakened and develops as the child reponds to the incidents of his childhood. All children possess powers of the imagination, and these, when allowed to develop naturally, provide the basis of our imaginative sympathy with our fellow men in later life.

Wordsworth thinks of the world and the mind as not being entirely separate, since there is no way of making available to us a world that has not been interpreted for us by our minds. This complicated doctrine, to which, in one form or another, most philosophers subscribe, is illustrated in many places in *The Prelude*.

The interaction of the human mind and the external world (that of 'Nature') is developed by Wordsworth into the belief that Nature, treated as though 'she' were a person, carefully educates the growing child by exercising his powers of imagination. Sometimes this education is carried forward in a gentle manner; on other occasions, as in the famous boat-stealing episode, Nature employs 'severer interventions'. Wordsworth's insistence that Nature has planned his adventure and is seeking to educate him is built into his description of it, which begins:

> One summer evening (led by her) I found
> A little boat tied to a willow tree.

The parenthetical comment is a reference to Nature. (In 'Resolution and Independence' Wordsworth describes his meeting with the leech-gatherer as being, perhaps, 'a *leading* from above, a something given'.)

Though the boat-stealing incident takes place on a summer evening when the days are long, Wordsworth indicates that it is growing dark ('glittering idly in the moon', 'the stars and the grey sky'). The child is alone, is taking a boat that does not belong to him, and is troubled in his conscience by what he is doing. At the same time, however, he is excited: 'It was an act of stealth/ And troubled pleasure'. The excitement, and his sense of daring and of wrong-doing, heighten the child's awareness of his surroundings and this enables Nature to teach him a lesson. (This last phrase, with its suggestion of reprimand as well as of education, is especially well suited to the mood of the passage.)

When he rows out on the lake the relationships that the hills seem to bear to each other change. As they do so a peak that had previously been hidden behind a nearer and smaller hill seems to rise up ('as if with voluntary power instinct') behind the child and to threaten him:

> from behind that craggy steep till then
> The horizon's bound, a huge peak, black and huge . . .
> Upreared its head.

The child begins to be afraid. 'I struck and struck again' means that he strikes his oars into the water in order to speed his boat, but suggests also the child's frightened lashing out against danger. As he rows further away from the peak, more and more of it is revealed, making it seem to be growing taller and to be pursuing him ('with purpose of its own . . . like a living thing').

That the child is allowing his guilty conscience to influence his interpretation of his surroundings becomes clearer if we compare with this incident the earlier one in which he steals woodcock. There again he is troubled ('anxious visitation'). It is late ('moon and stars/ Were shining o'er my head'), and he is alone ('I was alone'). And once again, even though he has not this time seen one hill looming up behind another, he both fears and imagines pursuit ('low breathings coming after me, and sounds/ Of undistinguishable motion').

The child lives in a world that is replete with moral values: notice how his sense of guilt inserts itself into a seemingly innocent line such as 'And through the silent water *stole* my way'. The child calls upon the whole of nature to picture for him his emotional distress, and is never a mere onlooker. The latter is what those adults who have lost contact with nature too often become. If, however, they remember their childhood and its lessons, they will never be able to regard themselves as isolated from their natural surroundings or from the rest of mankind.

Part 5

Suggestions for further reading

The text

The notes in the present volume are keyed to the following text:

Selections from Wordsworth: Poetry and Prose, edited by Ifor Evans, Methuen, London, 1935; eleventh edition, 1966.

The standard editions of the poetry, prose, and letters are:

Poetry:

The Poetical Works of William Wordsworth, edited by Ernest de Selincourt and Helen Darbishire, 5 vols, Clarendon Press, Oxford, 1940–9. This edition prints the last version of Wordsworth's texts to have been authorised, but lists earlier readings.

The Prelude, edited by Ernest de Selincourt, revised by Helen Darbishire, Clarendon Press, Oxford, 1959. This edition includes, on facing pages, the 1805 and 1850 texts.

Two paperback editions of *The Prelude* are also worth consulting. They are:

The Prelude: A Parallel Text, edited by J.C. Maxwell, Penguin Books, Harmondsworth, 1971.

The Prelude, 1799, 1805, 1850, edited by Jonathan Wordsworth, M.H. Abrams, and Stephen Gill, W.W. Norton, New York, 1979.

Four volumes in 'The Cornell Wordsworth' are of special interest. They include photographic reproductions of manuscripts as well as detailed transcriptions and reading-texts. Though primarily designed for advanced students, these volumes may be profitably consulted by any interested reader. They are:

The Salisbury Plain Poems, edited by Stephen Gill, Cornell University Press, Ithaca, New York; Harvester Press, Hassocks, Sussex, 1975.

The Prelude, 1798–1799, edited by Stephen Parrish, Cornell University Press, Ithaca, New York, 1977.

Home at Grasmere: Part First, Book First, of 'The Recluse', edited by Beth Darlington, Cornell University Press, Ithaca, New York, 1977.

'The Ruined Cottage' and 'The Pedlar', edited by James Butler, Cornell University Press, Ithaca, New York, 1979.

Prose:

The Prose Works of William Wordsworth, edited by W.J.B. Owen and Jane Worthington Smyser, 3 vols, Clarendon Press, Oxford, 1974.

Letters:
The six-volume edition of the Letters, edited by Ernest de Selincourt, is in the process of revision. The following revised volumes have appeared so far, under the general title of *The Letters of William and Dorothy Wordsworth*, Clarendon Press, Oxford, 1967 onwards. They are: *The Early Years, 1787–1805*, revised Chester L. Shaver (1967); *The Middle Years*, Part I, *1806–1811*, revised Mary Moorman (1969); *The Middle Years*, Part II, *1812–1820*, revised Mary Moorman and A.G. Hill (1970); *The Later Years*, Part I, *1821–1828*, revised A.G. Hill (1978); *The Later Years*, Part II, *1829–1834*, revised A.G. Hill (1979).

Early secondary works

COLERIDGE, SAMUEL TAYLOR: *Biographia Literaria*, edited by George Watson, Dent, London, 1956. A work of great interest, and of very considerable difficulty.

DE QUINCEY, THOMAS: *Recollections of the Lakes and the Lake Poets*, edited by David Wright, Penguin Books, Harmondsworth, 1970.

MILL, JOHN STUART: *Autobiography*, edited by Jack Stillinger, Oxford University Press, London, 1971.

WORDSWORTH, DOROTHY: *Journals of Dorothy Wordsworth*, edited by Ernest de Selincourt, 2 vols, Macmillan, London, 1941.

A useful collection of nineteenth- and twentieth-century views of Wordsworth will be found in:

MCMASTER, GRAHAM (ED.): *William Wordsworth: A Critical Anthology*, Penguin Books, Harmondsworth, 1972.

Less comprehensive, though still useful, is:

HARVEY, W.J. AND GRAVIL, RICHARD (ED.): *The Prelude: A Casebook*, Macmillan, London, 1972.

More recent secondary works

The best, fullest, and the most readable biography is the following:

MOORMAN, MARY: *William Wordsworth: A Biography*, 2 vols, Clarendon Press, Oxford, 1957–65.

Advanced students may also wish to consult:

REED, MARK: *Wordsworth: The Chronology of the Early Years, 1770–1799*, Harvard University Press, Cambridge, Massachusetts, 1967; and *Wordsworth: The Chronology of the Middle Years, 1800–1815*, Harvard University Press, Cambridge, Massachusetts, 1975.

Of other modern works the following can be recommended:

BATESON, F.W.: *Wordsworth: A Re-Interpretation*, Longman, London, 1954. Despite some biographical red herrings, this is a good and quite simple introduction to the poetry.

BEER, JOHN: *Wordsworth and the Human Heart*, Macmillan, London, 1978.

BYATT, A.S.: *Wordsworth and Coleridge in their Time*, Nelson, London, 1970. Illustrated.

DANBY, J.F.: *The Simple Wordsworth*, Routledge and Kegan Paul, London, 1960.

DARBISHIRE, HELEN: *The Poet Wordsworth*, Clarendon Press, Oxford, 1950. An uncomplicated introduction.

FORD, BORIS (ED.): *From Blake to Byron* ('The Pelican Guide to English Literature', 5), Penguin Books, Harmondsworth, 1957. This contains a good essay on Wordsworth and essays on his contemporaries and on 'The Social Setting' and 'The Character of Literature'. Especially recommended to students who are seeking an easy first introduction to the period.

HAVENS, R.D.: *The Mind of a Poet*, 2 vols, The Johns Hopkins Press, Baltimore, 1941.

JACOBUS, MARY: *Tradition and Experiment in Wordsworth's 'Lyrical Ballads'*, Clarendon Press, Oxford, 1976.

PARRISH, STEPHEN: *The Art of the Lyrical Ballads*, Harvard University Press, Cambridge, Massachusetts, 1973.

THOMPSON, T.W.: *Wordsworth's Hawkshead*, edited by Robert Woof, Oxford University Press, London, 1970. This is a superb book, detailed use of which is best left to advanced students.

TRILLING, LIONEL: 'The Immortality Ode' in *The Liberal Imagination: Essays on Literature and Society*, Secker and Warburg, London, 1951.

WORDSWORTH, JONATHAN: *The Music of Humanity*, Nelson, London, 1969.

WORDSWORTH, JONATHAN (ED.): *Bicentenary Wordsworth Studies in Memory of John Alban Finch*, Cornell University Press, Ithaca, New York, 1970.

The author of these notes

P.H. PARRY was educated in North Wales, and at the Universities of Bristol, Birmingham (The Shakespeare Institute), and St Andrews, where he is now a lecturer in English Literature. His doctoral dissertation was a study of Wordsworth's *A Guide through the District of the Lakes in the North of England.*